Happy You, Happy Family

Find Your Recipe for Happiness in the Chaos of Parenting Life

By Kelly Holmes

Third edition May 2017

ISBN 978-1537224466

To Tyler, for all the lunches and the dessert and the babies

Contents

Section 1
Introduction

1

The Day I Broke

I work from home with kids in tow. A toddler, an infant, and a second-grader who's admittedly pretty low maintenance, especially during the hours of 7:45 am to 2:45 pm. Working from home in your jammies *plus* more time with your kids sounds pretty awesome. Or at least it did to me from the outside looking in, and I do appreciate it most of the time.

But this setup comes with its own special challenges that test the limits of your patience. For example, when you lay your baby on your lap and prop your laptop behind her head so you can make eye contact every couple minutes but still get some work done, you'll learn that babies aren't dummies. She *knows* what you're doing, and she's going to let you hear it.

Or when you get up to change the baby's diaper and you leave your laptop on the living room end table, you'll come back to find that your toddler managed to delete your latest draft, tweet your grocery list, and disable your trackpad, which you didn't even realize was a thing.

And then you have the days when you reach your breaking point before 10:00 am, thanks to a Sharpie, a diaper blowout, and your toddler getting elbows deep in something toddlers should never, ever touch. But that's a story for another day. (Chapter 12 if you can't wait.)

Whether your main gig is managing the household, working from home, or leaving home to work in a cubicle – or some combination therein – parenting can be overwhelming. Frustrating. Maddening.

Finding happiness in the chaos of parenting life seems *impossible* most days. Until recently, I really did believe it was impossible.

Until the Day I Broke

I had resigned myself to the idea that in this season of motherhood, in order to get work done I'd have to manage to do two (or three) things at once. Entertain the baby while I answer email. Build a LEGO tower while I jot down ideas for my next blog post. Make the toddler's lunch while I bounce a fussy baby on my hip *and* pick away at editing photos for a post.

I told myself the kids would just have to deal with having a distracted, overwhelmed mom. We needed my income, we couldn't add childcare to our strict budget, and I had no other option for getting my work done.

And I'd pretty much accepted the reality of what would happen when I was focused on my work and something interrupted me.

Short answer? I lashed out like a bear. No, that's not accurate. I lashed out like a bear who hasn't slept three hours straight in three years because to her bear cubs, sleeping through the night is an *unspeakable* torture devised by mankind to inflict upon poor defenseless bear cubs.

I wasn't proud of lashing out, but a few things made me feel better about it:

- I wasn't yelling. "Just" snapping.
- I always caught myself and recovered quickly. Within 10 minutes, I was back on track.
- I'd promise myself I'd never do it again. And the rest of the day – even sometimes for two or three days – I was on my best behavior.

For whatever reason, this day was different. And yet, looking back on it, I see that this day was entirely unremarkable because it looked a lot like every other day.

I had a deadline to meet, but my newborn Charlie was having *none of it*. The only thing that kept her happy was walking around the house non-stop. Which isn't conducive to getting work done on a computer. And of course, she wouldn't sleep.

I sat her on my lap, held her with one hand while I bounced my knees up and down, and used the other hand to type using the extra efficient hunt-and-peck style.

She wasn't impressed with my multitasking. Her fusses turned into full-blown screeches every few minutes, so I'd stop and make eye contact and coo until she went back to a low-grade level of fussiness.

I checked the clock. If I didn't move fast, I wasn't going to finish my work by the deadline.

Hunt and peck, bounce the baby, hunt and peck, shush the baby.

And then my toddler Bailey must have gotten *bored* with the epic mess she'd created in the upstairs kids' room because I heard the thud of her steps coming down the stairs.

Side note: Ever since Bailey was a baby, the only way she'd fall asleep was if I was lying next to her and she could wrap her little fingers up in my hair. Even now when she's awake, she plays with my hair when she's upset, stressed, or needing an extra dose of connection.

On that day, Bailey's mom was distracted by work, her baby sister Charlie was crying, and nobody was paying attention to her.

Bailey sidled up next to me on the couch, one thumb in her mouth and the other fingers reaching for my hair.

Hunt and peck, bounce the baby, angle my head toward the toddler who's pulling my hair.

Check the clock. *I need to hurry.*

Hunt and peck, shush the baby, reach up to feel my hair.

"Bailey! You can't twist my hair into a knot." I let out a huff of frustration, then undid the knot before it was irreversible.

Hunt and peck, bounce the baby, angle my head.

And I could feel her twisting the hair again. Making another knot.

"Don't touch me!" And I reached my free hand out to push her away from me.

She started back towards me.

"I don't want you to touch me right now!" It was *too much*. The deadline. The fussy baby. The toddler literally pulling me in another direction. All at once.

"Mama?" Fear in her eyes.

"I need space!" Charlie's fusses turned to full-blown cries.

The corners of Bailey's mouth turned down. "But I need you!" The first tears rolled down her cheeks.

She started towards me again.

"I can't stand you touching me right now!" My heart felt like it was too big for my chest. Like it might explode.

I stood up, the baby in my arms, and walked to the master bedroom.

Charlie crying, Bailey following me while crying. "Mama! I need you!"

I set Charlie down in her crib, walked away from them both and toward the bathroom.

"Mama!"

I ignored her. Said *nothing* to my upset child.

I shut the bathroom door behind me, then walked to the closet and shut that door, too.

And I screamed.

I can't remember ever screaming in my adult life. My throat hurt, but I kept screaming.

When I ran out of breath, I panted. Like an animal.

I felt better, but I *didn't* feel better.

I wanted to scream again, but I *didn't* want to scream again.

I didn't want to let the raw emotion take control of my whole body again.

And I kind of...melted. I sunk to the floor, and heat pricked at my eyes. But I was too empty to cry real tears.

After the Storm

I took a deep breath. In with the clean, cool air. Out with the dirty, angry air.

With two closed doors between us, I could barely hear the two kids crying. But I did. And I knew they must have heard my scream.

Shame flooded my veins, and I wanted to curl up into a ball.

But I stood up and reached out for the closet door with a shaking hand.

Another deep breath, then I turned the knob.

Through the closet door and the bathroom door, then I scooped up the baby and pressed her head against my shoulder.

"Shh, shh, shh." Charlie gulped, and her cries went down an octave.

Bailey watched me. "Mama, you left and Charlie screamed." Her nose running, her cheeks glistening from the tears. Voice broken.

"I know," I whispered.

"Mama, I need you."

"I know." I bent down to Bailey's level and opened up my other arm to her for a hug.

She latched onto me in my awkward squat position, and Charlie's cries turned to whimpers.

All three of us held on for a long time.

Three Lessons

That day, I learned three lessons about finding happiness in the chaos of parenting life:

1. **I can't do it all.** My expectations of myself were too high. My to-do list was too long. It was impossible to get it all done.
2. **I can't "will" myself to be happier.** Every time I lost my temper, I deepened my resolve to never do it again. It didn't work. This was beyond mental brawn, and I needed help.
3. **I was really out of shape.** Holding a squat position for three minutes just about did me in.

Above all, I realized I had to make a change. And I admitted that the change had to be more than just *deciding* to be better next time.

So I did what I always do when life throws me for a loop. I researched. And researched. And researched some more.

How do you find happiness in the chaos of parenting?

Here's the Worst Part

There I was, completely overwhelmed with my life as a mom, cranky 99 percent of the time, and desperate for a solution.

And do you know what I found, most of all?

Make time for you!

Exercise more!

When you're on the verge of losing your temper, just take a deep breath!

...and on and on.

Gee, thanks, parenting experts. I'm at my breaking point – no, past it – and the experts give me more stuff to do on top of *everything else* I don't have time for. Or the deep breath advice – like I hadn't thought of that already. All the deep breath does is load me up with more steam to un-leash on my poor kid.

But I knew I wasn't alone in feeling overwhelmed by the chaos of parenting life. I get emails every day from parents who feel as lost as I was feeling on that day.

I didn't just need to solve this for me. I needed to find something to help you, too. And I knew there had to be a more workable solution than making us feel *more* overwhelmed or piling on *more* guilt.

That's how I discovered the secrets. Ten secrets *every* parent should know about being happy.

2

How to Use This Book

Before we get to the secrets every parent should know about being happy, we need to get on the same page. This book will help you create a personalized plan to find your own happiness sweet spot as a parent. Like a personal trainer but for happiness – and way less expensive.

But personal trainers don't lift the weight for you. You still have to do the hard work. Becoming your happiest, healthiest self will require three things of you:

- **You must want to change.** I know this is true because otherwise, you wouldn't have purchased this book. Still, we need to get super clear on this step first. Maybe you hate the look on your child's face when you lose your patience. Maybe you hate how you and your spouse feel like ships passing in the night. Or maybe you just want to be able to read a novel for 10 minutes without feeling guilty that you're not doing laundry or making dinner or tidying up the house. Whatever your "why" is, close your eyes and picture it. Write it down if you can. "I want to change because..."

- **You must know how to change.** This is where I will help you. Instead of heaping on more and more to-dos to stress you out, I'll share the simple (and fun) steps you can take to get the biggest bang for your happiness buck.

- **You must set yourself up for success.** Let's say you have a goal to eat healthier. But when you go the grocery store, you fill your cart with Oreos, Pringles, and three different flavors of Ben & Jerry's ice cream. Unless you plan to invite me over to devour the goodies – and I would totally take one for the team and help you out there – you aren't going to meet your goal because your environment is directly in opposition with your goal. This is another area I will help you with.

That last point is key. Because if I start giving you tips on how to carve out a happier life as a parent without you *first* having a system in place for handling what's already overwhelming you, you'll revolt on me.

This is why step one of the next section is essential.

How to Create Your Recipe for Happiness

Your recipe for finding happiness in the chaos of parenting life is yours and yours alone. Follow these steps to create your own personal recipe.

1. Follow the tips in Section 2 to build a system that sets you up for success. You'll also learn how to start new habits, break bad ones, and make a habit stick.
2. Now you're ready to create your own recipe for happiness. The ideas in Section 3 are your ingredients. Feel free to jump around in that section and try what speaks to you. You may need to try a few different happiness habits until you find the perfect recipe for your happiness.
3. Use the bonus printable workbook included with your purchase of this book to keep track of what you end up loving. You'll also find a template for recording your personal recipe for happiness, plus more goodies to help you in your journey. Claim your workbook at idealistmom.com/happy-you-bonus.

When building your recipe, aim to find 3-5 activities that make the biggest impact to your daily happiness. This is not to say that you have to do all these *every day*.

Still, you will have the greatest success if you promise yourself to build habits for as many ingredients from your recipe as possible. (More on that in Section 2.)

However, as you'll soon learn, even if you do all this, you'll still have days where you lose your patience. Section 4 gives you a toolkit of proven tools to get you back on track.

Ready? Let's do this.

Download Your Bonus Workbook

As a bonus with this book, you also get access to a companion workbook of all the printables and worksheets mentioned in this book. This bonus workbook will help you find your *own* personal recipe for happiness in the chaos of parenting life. Here's how to get your bonus:

1. Claim your bonus workbook at idealistmom.com/happy-you-bonus.
2. Download the workbook PDF.
3. Print the workbook. You can even throw it in a cute binder if you want. I personally like to take advantage of any excuse for getting pretty new office supplies!

Section 2
Set Yourself up for Success

3

The First (and Most Important) Secret

W hen you read this first secret you should know about being a happy parent, it won't *look* like a secret. You'll read it, say "yeah yeah" in your head and keep reading to find something you haven't heard before.

But that would be a big mistake. Because giving lip service to this first secret would be the *opposite* of setting yourself up for success. It'd be like stocking your pantry with junk food when you want to eat healthier. First, let's talk about our expectations:

- You want to be a loving parent who guides your kids toward a life of happiness and success.
- You want to be a supportive partner who listens and does your fair share around the house and surprises your honey with sweet demonstrations of your love.
- You want to be a rockstar at work, surpassing all your goals and wowing your colleagues with your awesomeness.
- You want to help out at your kid's school, or start volunteering, or pick up a new hobby because it sounds fun but also because you read that trying something new is good for preventing Alzheimer's and you'd really like to avoid that if at all possible.

And more and more and more. Maybe all of the above, even.

But Here's the Deal

To meet your expectations of yourself, you'd need 48 hours in a day, and that doesn't include any time for sleep. So here's what happens:

1. Those expectations and to-do items swirl around in your head throughout the day. Every time you think of something, your stress level goes *up a notch*, like going up one notch on a roller coaster. For every time you think of something you should be doing but aren't, up you go. This low hum of stress is something your kids and partner can feel, too. They may not even be able to articulate it, but they can sense it. You keep going up one more notch and one more notch until you get to the top of the roller coaster...

2. You lose your patience. This looks different for every parent. Some of us yell. Some of us withdraw into silence. Some of us get a snippy tone. Or some combination of all three. You're flying down the biggest dip on the roller coaster, out of control. However this manifests in you, it's not a fun roller coaster to be on. And it *certainly* doesn't feel like how a happy parent would act.

3. You regroup. You catch yourself mid-descent or feel the thud of landing at the bottom. You might take a deep breath. Maybe you apologize to your kids or your partner. Sometimes you decide to take it easy and recharge – treat yourself to binge-watching your favorite show on Netflix or a few rounds of Candy Crush. You might even make a plan. "Next time, I won't lose my cool." And maybe next time, you do keep it together. But *meanwhile*, your high expectations are still swirling around in your head. One notch up, one notch up, one notch up. Until...

You're back at the top of the roller coaster again, on the brink of another free-fall.

My friend, it's time to get off the roller coaster. And the first secret is going to show you the way off.

Please read the next line out loud. If your toddler or your cat looks at you funny, no worries. This is important.

"I can't do it all."

Did you say it? I'm serious. I'll wait.

"I can't do it all."

Because that's the first secret every parent should know about being happy.

1. You Can't Do It All

Your expectations of yourself are too high. You're keeping a pantry full of Cocoa Puffs and expecting to end up with abs of steel.

And not only are your expectations too high, the swirling chaos of to-do items and appointments and "should"s in your head is adding to your stress.

Your short-term memory is not a USB drive. It's more like a magnifying glass. This means that you can think of only two or three things at once before you get distracted by your own mental load. A distracted parent is a parent who gets *frustrated* easily.

One of the best things you can do to cut down on overwhelm as a parent? Write everything you want to do in one place:

- You can use a planner, an app on your phone, or an Excel spreadsheet on your computer. It doesn't matter which one, but pick *one* single place.
- Whatever you choose, it needs to be something you have easy access to update when tasks pop into your head. To stop feeling overwhelmed, you must get everything out of your head and into one single repository.
- My personal preference is to use Evernote as my official master to-do list – linked at the end of this chapter. Evernote is an app where you keep one master list you can access on your phone or computer – or both. I always have my phone with me, so I always have my master list with me, too.

Bottom line: Make one master list of everything you want to do or need to do. When a new task pops into your head, add it to your master list as fast as humanly possible. The faster you can get it down on paper (actual or metaphorical), the happier your brain will be.

Do It Now

1. Decide where you'll keep your master to-do list. You'll find a link to a few options at the end of this chapter.
2. Set a timer for five minutes – a kitchen timer or the timer app on your phone would both work.
3. Hit start and for the next five minutes, write down every to-do and every "should" that comes to mind.
4. When the timer's up if you still have more swirling to-dos, set it for another five minutes and go again. If you think of something an hour later, add it to the list. If you're lying in bed and can't sleep because you thought of something you need to do, add it to the list so you can sleep!

Maybe you're thinking this sounds too simple. Maybe you're thinking you don't need this step. Maybe you were looking for a silver bullet to help you wake up tomorrow as the hap-hap-happiest parent who ever poured your kid's bowl of cereal at 5:02 a.m.

It's possible you don't need this step, of course. But in our chronically busy culture, I have yet to meet a fellow parent who can't rattle off 10 things they need to do or "should" be doing. So humor me. It'll take only 5 minutes.

You Might Hate Me for This

After you get your list out of your head and all in one place, your brain will sigh from the relief of not having to remember all those random tidbits.

But oh goodness, is that list overwhelming! Which is the *opposite* of the effect we're going for. The truth is your list is too long.

With too much weighing on you, you might try to do two or three things at the same time to get a bunch done. But when you're in multitasking mode and your kid asks for help with her homework or for a snack or why her friend Julie gets her own iPad but she has to share with her little sister, you'll be distracted. And remember: A distracted parent is an easily frustrated parent.

Maybe you've even noticed this about yourself and stopped multi-tasking, which is great. Even so, your list is *still* too long.

When you look at that long list, you might think: "I'll have more time later." When the kids are back in school after the break, when you finish that big project at work, when when when...

Wrong. Research on time perceptions shows that we typically imagine we'll be less busy in the future. But we're mistaken. Later is like a mirage in the desert. When you get there, you realize it was a trick of the mind, and now your list is even longer.

Stop telling yourself you'll have more time later. It's a lie. For all those things you think you'll get to "one day," you probably won't. And every time you push something out in your mind, you'll be disappointed in yourself. Those undone tasks will weigh you down.

What I'm about to ask you to do is hard. *So hard.* My husband keeps me honest with this particular step, and anytime he calls me on it, I huff like a moody teenager.

I never *want* to do this, and yet after I do, I can breathe again. So if you read the next section and groan a little (or a lot), please bear with me. Go through the steps. After you do, you'll be happy you did.

Do It Now

1. Grab your master list.
2. Okay, ready? Now find *one thing* you can take off the list. Yes, I really do mean delete it. Scratch through it until you can't read it anymore. If you're hyperventilating at the idea of doing this, I get it. I feel that way, too. Every time. But when you have more on your list than is humanly possible to get done, it adds to your stress. This is because those things you feel that you *should* do just sit on the list and sit on the list and never get done. You'll feel like a failure. **And you know what?** You're a busy parent raising tiny people to thrive in the world. You bought a book because you want to find a happier balance in your life. Failures don't do *that*. So don't let a bloated to-do list make you feel like a failure.
3. If this is as hard for you to do as it is for me, I have a couple tips to help you. For each item on your list, ask yourself **these two questions**. And if the answer is "no" to both, that item is probably a good candidate for deleting.
   - "Will finishing this spark joy?" Sometimes the joy that a task sparks isn't direct, but it's still there if you look. For example, setting up a backup drive for your computer doesn't sound particularly joyful. But the relief of knowing all your digital photos of your family are safe probably does spark joy.
   - "Is this essential?" For example, you might prefer to skip out on an evening conference call for work, but to get your work done you need information you'll get in that meeting. This would be an essential task.
4. If you really can't bring yourself to delete something from your list, **make a new list** called "Someday/Maybe" and move it to that. If you do reach that magical "one day" when the kids are playing independently and the laundry hamper is empty, whip out your Someday/Maybe list and go nuts. Or as another idea: In my family, we started making one

"Someday/Maybe" day every month where we pick som
thing we want to do "one day" and just start it.

5. After you cut something from your list, *do it again*. And
again and again until you truly can't bear to cut anymore.
This will be so hard, but if you want to make room in your
life for the things that will bring you greater happiness as a
parent, you must find that room somewhere.

This exercise is something you will want to complete on a *regular basis*. You can set yourself a reminder to do it once a month, or just do it every time you can feel the stress of your list starting to overwhelm you.

Are you cursing my name yet? I hope not, but I'll understand if you are. After you read the next tip, we'll be buds again.

This One Trick Will Make You Feel Like a Rockstar

If you take nothing else from this book, take this tip and use it every single stinkin' day. It's *that* good.

To recap: You have a master list that lives outside your head, *and* you've culled it to *only* the essential tasks and/or the things that will bring you joy.

But here's the problem. You can't work from this list. Even if you color-coded it to death, your master list is too big, unwieldy, and overwhelming.

In fact, try not to think of your master list as a to-do list. Think of it as a *parking lot* for all the thoughts zooming around in your brain.

The solution? *MITs*. Otherwise known as Most Important Tasks.

Every morning, this is the first thing you should do before you check email or read the news: Look at your master list, and pick three tasks that are most important to get done that day, and jot them down. Or if you prefer, you can pick your MITs the night before.

The key is to pick the three things that *must* happen today. And if you finish your MITs for the day, you can officially consider yourself a rockstar.

I can hear you right now. *"But…three? Just THREE?!? You're a madwoman."* Yes, *just* three.

If your daily to-do list has more than three MITs, the danger is that when you look at your list or think of it, you'll feel overwhelmed and procrastinate the whole thing. Decision overload is a real thing, and you don't want to run into it every time you look at your priorities for the day.

You can always do more than your MITs, but do those first. Before you play a round of Angry Birds or schedule that overdue dentist appointment – do your MITs. (I'm tempted to suggest you do them even before your first cup of coffee, but I don't want hate mail from your family. Still, that gives you an idea of exactly how important it is to do your MITs first.)

Here's the beauty of MITs: You'll feel infinitely better about how much you're getting done, plus when you get a few minutes free time you'll be focused on your top priorities instead of getting distracted by the chime of the latest Facebook notification.

Your MITs give you a *roadmap* for your day. If you end up with 20 extra minutes where your kids or your spouse or the cat aren't bugging you for something, now you know exactly what to work on. You don't end up wasting your available time, floundering around trying to decide what to do.

Keep in mind that MITs should be tasks, not huge projects. More along the lines of "Go through the mail on the counter" and not "Purge junk from every closet in the house." Also, you don't need to use up an MIT slot for something that's already an established habit or routine. No need to write down "Brush my teeth" or "Make dinner." For example, here are my MITs from the other day:

1. Reserve a spot at the dog boarder for our vacation in a few weeks
2. Return a present that didn't fit
3. Design a printable MIT sheet (more on that in a minute)

I did the first with my morning coffee, ran a mid-morning errand for the second, then I picked away at the third in short bursts whenever I ended up with free time.

You'll have a new set of MITs every day, so feel free to use whatever works: a Post-It note, your phone, or the back of a Costco receipt.

Included in your bonus companion workbook, you'll find a printable MIT template just for you. After you download and print the workbook, you can cut it to make enough MIT sheets for four days: idealistmom.com/happy-you-bonus.

Do It Now

1. Grab a scrap of paper or your phone – or print the MIT template included with this book.
2. Looking at your master list, pick your three MITs for today (or tomorrow) and write them down.
3. And the most important step: At the end of the day, pitch your list of MITs so you *start fresh* the next day. If one of your MITs was something new that's not on your master list and you didn't finish it that day, add it to the master list and then throw away your MIT list for the day.

In the next chapter, we'll get to the rest of the secrets every parent should know about being happy. But first, let's review what we've covered so far.

3 Must-Dos to Avoid Overwhelm

1. Keep a master list of all the to-dos and "should"s and commitments swirling around in your brain. Add to it anytime you think of something new.
2. On a regular basis, cull your list to essential tasks and/or those that bring you joy. Keep a secondary Someday/Maybe list if it's too hard to delete items.
3. Every morning, start by making your list of three MITs for the day. *Just three.*

Supplies You'll Need

- A single place to keep your master list – a planner, an app on your phone, or an Excel spreadsheet on your computer. My personal favorite is Evernote, and Google Keep is a newer option that has similar functionality. Learn about them and download at idealistmom.com/happy-you-resources.
- A timer – a kitchen timer or the timer app on your phone would both work.
- A scrap of paper or your phone so you can jot down your MITs every morning – or print the MIT template included with this book.

4

9 More Secrets You Must Accept

Maybe your patience seems to disappear when your kids test the boundaries. Maybe you know you need "me time" but can't seem to make it happen. Or you might feel overwhelmed with everything that you *should* be doing to keep your family trucking along.

Remember the first secret.

1. You Can't Do It All

The system you put in place in the last chapter will help you keep your high expectations in check: a parking lot for what pops into your head, a Someday/Maybe list, and your daily MITs.

Now it's time to set the record straight with *9 more secrets* about finding happiness in the chaos of parenting.

When I first encountered each of these, I didn't want to believe them. They didn't fit with my preconceived notions of how the world works. But each of these secrets is backed by science, so I started paying more attention to how each situation played out in my own life.

If you read one of the secrets and think, "That's hogwash," I get it. And I would have agreed with you not too long ago. But I also know that we humans have a fundamental bias against new information that doesn't fit with our existing world view. So in my research, I *forced* myself to keep an open mind. I approached the subject of my own happiness as a curious student. By the way, that reminds me of one of my favorite quotes ever:

"Live your life as a curious student and you will discover how fascinating it is." – Elena Ornig

Ready with an open mind? Let's get back to the secrets every parent should know about being happy.

2. You Can't "Will" Yourself to Be Happier

In Chapter 1, I shared the story of the Day I Broke. My lowest point as a parent. Until that day, I was caught in this cycle:

- Get progressively more annoyed and frustrated by little things until I lose my patience with my kids.
- Set my jaw a little bit tighter and promise myself a little more vehemently to never blow up again.
- Rinse and repeat.

But after I hit my lowest point, I realized I needed help. And my research soon showed me where I'd gone wrong.

As it turns out, you have limited reserves of willpower that drain as each day goes on. This is why when people set goals to eat healthier but they end up cheating, it usually happens at the end of the day when their resolve is weakened.

In fact, relying on your willpower tires you out. In one study, researchers placed people in a room with freshly baked cookies and told them they couldn't eat the cookies. Nobody gave in – although I surely would have.

Another group was put in a room with a bunch of radishes and told they couldn't eat the vegetables, but they could have all the cookies they wanted – no willpower necessary there. Then the researchers gave everyone a test that couldn't be solved, but the subjects didn't know that. The lucky folks who got to eat cookies kept trying on their tests for an average of 19 minutes. The people who had to use up their willpower to not eat the cookies? They gave up after only 8 minutes.

Your limited willpower is also why you can read article after article about how to find more happiness and not ever see a real change. You need *more* than just a promise to yourself for real change to happen. So now you will understand why we spent the last chapter putting a system in place.

If your goal is to be a happier parent, you need more than just a firm resolve. And that's why I wrote this book – to share the other piece of the equation with you.

3. Venting Can Be Dangerous

When I had a particularly bad day and my husband got home from work, the minute he walked in the door, I'd unleash, looking to him for validation. He listened and validated my emotions, every time.

But I had to admit: Sharing my frustrations did nothing to make my frustration and anger go away. In fact, afterwards, I felt the heels of my anger dig deeper into the earth.

Later, I learned that there's a *reason* I didn't feel better after venting to my husband. Venting isn't a great way to dissolve anger. It's actually a horrible idea if you really want to stop being angry and get happy again.

What does work? It depends on the person. After you build your personal recipe for happiness, use the toolkit in Section 4 to prepare for those moments so you can catch yourself from falling into the angry abyss.

4. Your Moods Are Catching

Research shows the bad mood of one person can bring down the mood of everyone else in the family.

I don't say this to stress you out about the times when you're struggling to get back to a happy place. However, when I realized that the *whole family* would benefit from me finding happiness, that elevated my project from a personal goal to a family goal. If it helps you to know this too, I wanted to share this tidbit.

5. Parents Need Recess, Too

You probably already realize you need "me time." I did, too.

But who has time for that when you can barely keep up with house-work, all the kids' needs and wants, keeping the spark alive with your partner, meeting expectations for work, and and and...? But here's the thing:

- You are *not* a computer. You are not designed to run at high speeds being super productive for long stretches of time.
- All the tasks and decisions you make throughout the day wear on your brain.
- You *must* give your brain a chance to recuperate so you don't get burned out or turn into the Incredible Hulk when your kid inter-rupts you to ask for help with her homework.

My first attempt at making "me time" last summer was an epic fail-ure. **Why?** Because sometimes when you think you're doing something to recharge, it's not actually recharging your batteries at all.

What you do during your "me time" matters. For example, binge-watching your favorite TV show on Netflix doesn't really help your brain recuperate from the stresses of the day. We'll talk more about the best kind of "me time" in Chapter 7.

6. You Can't Control Your Kids

In a large percentage of the situations where I lose patience with my kids, I get frustrated because they aren't doing what I want them to do. And I'm not alone. For a lot of parents, *power struggles* rank at the top of daily frustrations. For example:

- When we need to leave the house at a certain time to make an ap-pointment, and the toddler refuses to brush her teeth.
- Or when I ask my 7-year-old to put away her laundry, and she doesn't hear me because her nose is buried in a book.
- Or like last night at 2:00 am when my baby just. wouldn't. sleep.

Life as a parent has taught me that ultimately, I *can't* force my kids to do what they don't want to do. Anyone who's ever lived through non-napping days with toddlers knows this. And when you do strong-arm your kid into doing something they really and truly do not want to do, they will usually find a way around it. Maybe not today, but one day.

What's more, kids need to be open to the idea of learning a lesson, or nothing will stick. Fear and shame shut down the part of the brain that can learn those lessons. When I lose my cool with my kids, I'm actually cementing the fact that they won't learn *a darn thing* from the situation.

When I accept this and stop trying to control every little thing, I'm an entirely different mom. I'm playful. I smile more. My kids surprise me with heartfelt, spontaneous "I love you"s that melt me.

If the power struggles feel like an endless game of tug-of-war, make a decision to gently lay down your end of the rope. You don't need to dig in your heels to make a point with your kid. Pretend your little one is just a friend who needs help dealing with the situation.

7. 100% Is Impossible

Let's say you set a goal to eat healthier. And you know that if you stock your pantry with Cheetos and Twinkies, you probably won't stick to your goal.

Because your environment – your system – wouldn't support your goal. This is why we spent the last chapter setting up a system to keep you on track. You have your master list, your three MITs every day, and maybe even a Someday/Maybe list. This is the *equivalent* of keeping your pantry free of junk food.

But now let's suppose you're volunteering at the annual fundraiser for your kid's school. A fundraiser that happens to include a bake sale. You *resist the urge* for the first hour of your shift, but then you just can't take it anymore.

You buy a cookie.

And you eat it. And it's delicious.

As the last bite hits your mouth, the guilt sets in. *"Why did I do that? I was doing so well. Now I blew it."*

But you would be *wrong*. You didn't blow it because you ate one cookie.

What blows your healthy eating goal is thinking *one slip-up* is a failure, so then you decide you might as well eat another cookie. And another and another and another.

Why am I talking about cookies?

Aside from the fact that I have the most voracious sweet tooth known to all of mankind, you mean?

Here's why: You set a goal to become your happiest, healthiest self. And you are on the right track. You're trying new things. Seeing what works for you and your family. You're *living* your commitment to happiness.

But there *will* come a time when you slip up. Because your willpower is limited. This isn't something to feel guilty about because it's human nature. Fancy brain science has proven this fact.

One day, your reserves of willpower will hit empty. You're running late but someone moved your car keys and you can't find them. Or you didn't set your MITs first thing in the morning. Or maybe you snapped at your kids. Or yelled.

You are not a failure.

One slip-up is not a failure. A slip-up followed by stopping all these science-backed habits and systems that I'm sharing with you? *That* would be a failure.

If your goal is to reach happiness 100 percent of the time, your goal is unrealistic. Nobody is happy 100 percent of the time.

Because 100 percent is impossible.

Don't make the mistake of letting one slip-up pull you back on the roller coaster cycle that leads to unhappiness.

No matter how many healthy habits and systems you put in place, you *will* encounter small frustrations and annoyances every day. And you can't deal with them by denying that you feel frustrated or annoyed.

Because that would make it *worse*.

In fact, the faster you can recognize a negative emotion, the faster you can move on from it. More on this in Section 4.

8. You Are Not Alone

Remember: You must want to change, you must know how to change, and you must set yourself up for success.

You bring the first ingredient to the table, and I've been helping you with the second and third.

By now, you've seen it is possible to find more happiness as a parent. We haven't even got to Section 3 yet, but I've already shared a few simple steps you can take towards your goal to be a happier parent. But because you are forming new habits, sticking to them will take *community*.

In my research, I came across this nugget in a book called *The Power of Habit*:

"When people join groups where change seems possible, the potential for that change to occur becomes more real. For most people who overhaul their lives, there are no seminal moments or life-altering disasters. There are simply communities—sometimes of just one other person—who make change believable."

To become your happiest, healthiest self, you need a community of parents taking this journey with you. This is why the purchase of this book includes access to a private Facebook community of your fellow parents on the *Happy You, Happy Family* path.

9. Happiness Is Habits

I have another quote for you, from Elizabeth Gilbert in *Eat, Pray, Love*:

"Happiness is the consequence of personal effort. You fight for it, strive for it, insist upon it, and sometimes even travel around the world looking for it. You have to participate relentlessly in the manifestations of your own blessings. And once you have achieved a state of happiness, you must never become lax about maintaining it. You must make a mighty effort to keep swimming upward into that happiness forever, to stay afloat on top of it."

I love this quote, but it's also kind of frustrating.

Because it sure would be nice to put "Be happy" on your to-do list, mark it off, and never have to worry about it again.

The truth is that Elizabeth Gilbert is *spot on*. Happiness is not a checkbox. And it can take a good deal of personal effort to find happiness in the chaos of parenting.

But when you're already overwhelmed with commitments and to-dos and your own high expectations, that fact can be pretty stressful.

Here's the *good news*. In my research, I found the secret to making this constant struggle toward happiness not quite so constant and not so much of a struggle.

Happiness still isn't a checkbox, but happiness *is* habits. Remember how you have limited reserves of willpower? You can't "will" yourself to be happier because when your willpower is tapped, your patience will be too. The answer to finding more patience isn't to try harder.

The answer is habit. The more you can make something habitual, the *less effort* it will take. You don't have to try with all your might to brush your teeth every day because it's a habit. It's not a chore to lock the door when you leave the house because it's a habit. It isn't a daily struggle to remember to say "good morning" to your kid when she wakes up because it's a habit.

This is why in the next chapter, we'll talk about habits – how to start new habits, how to break bad ones, and how to make a habit stick. Writing down your three MITs every morning is one habit, and you'll want to build more happiness habits to reach your goal.

Happiness won't come from a big promotion at work, or from winning the lottery, or from your kids all learning to put their toys away when they're done playing.

Because eventually, you just get used to all that stuff. True, lasting happiness comes from a conscious effort *by you* to put the right habits in place.

The right daily habits serve as a steward of your happiness. They're like giving yourself an Iron Man suit against all the frustrations and annoyances of parenting life.

10. Your Happy Is Your Happy

For one mom, planning her family's meals ahead of time keeps her from feeling frazzled. But others may enjoy the spontaneity of pulling together dinner from whatever's on hand in the fridge.

One dad might enjoy reading to his kids, while other parents might connect with their little ones through some healthy roughhousing.

Or you may find that sketching and doodling fills your happiness tank, whereas I can't draw a stick figure to save my life, so that wouldn't be a good fit for me.

Your recipe for finding happiness in the chaos of parenting life is yours and yours alone.

Nothing works for 100 percent of people 100 percent of the time. You might not be a hugger, or your partner may look at you funny when you try to start a gratitude ritual at dinnertime. Happiness habits are not one-size-fits-all.

To find your own personal recipe for happiness, you'll need to try a few different habits and see how they fit you and your family.

Use Section 3 to do just that, plus you can print the printable chart included with your bonus companion workbook to keep track of what you've tried and what you've loved. Download your bonus workbook at idealistmom.com/happy-you-bonus.

The Secrets, One Last Time

1. You can't do it all. (No, really. I mean it.)
2. You can't "will" yourself to be happier.
3. Venting can be dangerous.
4. Your moods are catching.
5. Parents need recess, too.
6. You can't control your kids.
7. 100% is impossible.
8. You are not alone.
9. Happiness is habits.
10. Your happy is your happy.

5

Build the Right Habits

Your willpower is a finite resource, so you can't rely on your mental resolve to help you find more happiness in the chaos of parenting life.

The answer? Happiness habits.

Habits work because they put your brain on autopilot. You don't have to use up your reserves of willpower to stay happy all day when you have the right habits because they set you up for success.

But forming a new habit isn't always easy.

How many times have you set a goal – to exercise more, or to eat healthier, or to stop watching *Friends* re-runs on Netflix so you can get to bed at a decent hour – only to revert back to the status quo after a couple weeks or months?

If your answer is "never" and you rock at forming new habits that stick, feel free to skip this chapter and move along in your happiness journey. But if you've ever struggled to stick with new habits, this chapter will give you science-backed tools to ease the habit-forming process.

You won't need to use *all* these tricks for every new habit, but you're likely to experience greater success if you can find a way to use more than one technique as you're forming a new habit.

Read this chapter through once, then when it's time to develop a plan for a new happiness habit, use the cheat sheet of questions at the end of this chapter to refresh your memory and decide which tools you'll use.

Side note: You can use all the tools in this chapter to form *any* new habit – not just the happiness habits you'll find in this book.

But First, A Caveat

You're ready for a change. That's why you bought this book.

But resist the urge to tackle a bunch of new habits all at once. You'll have the greatest success if you try one new habit at a time. And not just that, but you'll be most successful if you try one new, *small* habit at a time.

Forming a new habit requires willpower, and you already know your willpower is limited. If you decide to start five new habits on Monday, you'll use up your willpower with the first habit, be unable to follow through on the other four habits, and feel like a failure. Every time you set yourself up for failure in this way, you make it harder to try again the next day.

Bundle the Temptation

This trick works best for habits that aren't necessarily your idea of a good time. For me, the thought of exercising daily makes me whine like a hangry three-year-old. That makes a daily exercise habit a good fit for temptation bundling.

I like to think of this one as the peanut butter and jelly trick. Eating a heaping spoonful of peanut butter would make your mouth painfully dry. But mix it with a little jelly, and it's the perfect quick snack. Here's how temptation bundling works:

1. Pick a habit you'd like to start. This is the peanut butter.
2. Figure out something you love to do that you could bundle with that new habit. And this is the jelly.

For example, suppose I want to start a daily exercise habit (peanut butter). Something I love to do is read fiction (jelly). I could bundle a new exercise habit with reading. To do that, I would allow myself to read fiction *only* while on the treadmill at the gym, or I would listen to an audiobook *only* while I'm on a walk around the neighborhood.

This is the key: The only time I'm allowed to do the desirable activity (reading) is when I'm doing the undesirable activity (exercising). A few more examples for you:

- Listen to your favorite music album *only* while you clean
- Enjoy your morning cup of coffee *only* while you set the day's MITs (see Chapter 3 for a refresher on MITs)
- Watch your favorite weekly television show *only* after you pay the bills

Take Advantage of the Fresh Start Effect

By nature, you're more open to making changes on the first day of the year, on the first of the month, or at the start of a new week. This is due to the *fresh start effect*.

When you're starting a new habit, pick a day that feels like a fresh start to you, whether it's your birthday, a Monday, or the first day of your kid's summer vacation.

Tweak Your Environment

Sometimes making a small change to your environment can take a lot of the hard work out of starting a new habit or breaking an old habit. When your environment supports your habit goals, you don't need to rely so much on your limited reserves of willpower.

Let's say during family dinners you tend to keep your phone next to your plate. When a notification pops up, you pick up your phone to check real quick but get roped into a text conversation or scrolling Facebook. Your partner starts telling a story from their day, but you're not giving them 100 percent of your attention. You look up and realize they're waiting on you for a response, but you're not sure what the question was.

The disappointment in your partner's eyes, night after night when this happens – that motivates you to make a change. But no matter how hard you try to avoid looking at the notifications, you can't help yourself.

The solution is to tweak your environment. For example, you might:

- Turn your phone to vibrate.
- Flip your phone upside down so you can't see the screen.
- Leave your phone in a kitchen drawer during dinner.

Any of those small environment tweaks would lead to you paying closer attention to your partner during family dinners.

Tweaking the environment is also a helpful technique for changing other people's behaviors. If your kid drives you crazy by leaving her dirty clothes all over her bedroom floor, she's most likely not doing it just to get on your nerves.

But maybe it would help to put a laundry hamper in her room. Or if she already has a laundry hamper in her room, is it hidden in a closet or in a corner behind a door? You could try moving it somewhere more visible.

These tweaks aren't meant to excuse your kid for not putting dirty clothes where they belong. But your kid has limited willpower, too. It doesn't hurt to grease the wheels a bit.

No promises that tweaking the environment will help with every annoying behavior in your house, but it's always worth a try.

Decide on an Action Trigger

Suppose you want to start a gratitude ritual with your family.

Decide on an action to trigger the new habit, and you'll cement that new habit in no time. For example, you might decide that when you sit down for family dinner, you'll ask the person next to you, "What are you grateful for?" The action of sitting down to dinner triggers the gratitude habit.

Deciding ahead of time when you'll do something pre-loads the decision, saving your limited willpower.

As another example, if you want to start a daily meditation habit, you might tell yourself, "After I brush my teeth at night, I'll meditate for 10 minutes."

Give Yourself a Cue

This is one of my favorite habit hacks, and it works especially well when you pair it with an action trigger. The trick is to make sure you keep changing it up.

Set up a visual cue to remind yourself of the habit when you're most likely to forget it.

Taking the gratitude ritual at dinner as an example, you might forget your pre-loaded decision to ask, "What are you grateful for?" and instead jump right into the elaborate song-and-dance required to get your toddler to eat her broccoli. This is where a visual cue comes in handy:

1. Find something a little out of the ordinary in your house and put it on your dinner table. It should be something you wouldn't expect to find on your dinner table. For example, you could get the hand mixer from the kitchen, your hair dryer, or that clay sculpture your big kid made at school that's supposed to be a leafy sea dragon but looks more like a clump of cat litter.
2. At dinnertime, when you sit down with your family, you'll think, "What the heck is that leafy sea dragon doing on the dinner table?" This is a *good* thing. Because...
3. That's your reminder to ask the question, "What are you grateful for?"
4. Leave the leafy sea dragon on your dinner table so you remember to do it again the next night and the next.

But here's the problem with visual cues: After a while, they become wallpaper. Once you get used to seeing the cue in your environment, the cue stops reminding you.

You can get around this by changing the cue itself or by putting it in a different location.

For example, let's talk about a nightly meditation habit. You could put a sticky note on your bathroom mirror to remind you to meditate after brushing your teeth. When the sticky note stops grabbing your attention, you could borrow your kid's washable window markers to write a reminder directly on the mirror.

Form a Supporting Habit

For hefty new habits, you might find it useful to form a smaller supporting habit first.

One helpful rule of thumb is to form a supporting habit that will get you 20 seconds closer to your main goal.

Let's say you tend to run late in the mornings, and you want to start leaving on time. A classic example of a supporting habit would be setting your clothes out the night before or making your kids' lunches the previous night – or both. For a supporting habit to be successful, it must be:

1. Relatively easy to do. If your supporting habit is just as hard as the main habit, you haven't gained an advantage.
2. Helpful in meeting your main goal. For example, if your goal is to leave the house on time in the morning, making the family freshly squeezed orange juice every morning wouldn't be a helpful supporting habit.

Rely on a Checklist

I once read an entire book about the power of checklists – if that gives you any idea of how type-A I am.

Checklists sometimes get a bad rap as bureaucratic or annoying, but the truth is that simple checklists have made people rich. Checklists build skyscrapers that don't fall down. Checklists save *lives*.

You probably already use some sort of checklist in your daily life. A grocery list is a checklist that helps you remember what you need from the store. A list of errands you need to run is a checklist. Even a recipe is a type of checklist.

From pilots to doctors to architects, people with important jobs rely on checklists for the simple reason that they *work*.

And what job is more important than raising a future citizen of the world? Checklists can help you stick to your happiness habits.

In fact, the printable template included with your bonus companion workbook is just that – a checklist for your personal recipe for happiness. The recipe you create and post somewhere visible is a tangible reminder of the steps you need to go through each day in order to achieve happiness amidst the chaos of parenting life. Download your bonus workbook at idealistmom.com/happy-you-bonus.

Another example that might be helpful is a morning routine checklist. If you tend to run late in the morning – or you find yourself endlessly nagging your straggling gaggle of kids to hurry up – and that sets your mood off for the whole day, a checklist could take a lot of the annoyance out of your morning. You might even have one checklist for the kids that they can mark off as they move through the morning, and another checklist to keep you on track.

Lean on Your Community

Remember this secret to happiness from Chapter 4?

You are not alone.

When you're a member of a community united by a common goal, your belief in the possibility of meeting that goal deepens. You see examples of others in the community making changes, and those changes become more doable in your mind. Who you spend time with influences you on a daily basis.

This is why the purchase of this book includes access to a private Facebook community of your fellow parents who are working toward the goal of finding more happiness. To make the most of this habit hack, share in the group when you achieve a happiness win. Post when you stumble. Pay it forward to other parents by cheering them on.

If Facebook isn't your thing, you can still harness the power of community in forming new happiness habits. Tell your family what you're trying to do. Or find a friend who's interested in making a change too, and agree to check in on each other.

Your New Habit Toolkit

1. **Bundle the temptation.** Can you find a way to attach the new habit to something that you love to do?
2. **Take advantage of the fresh start effect.** Can you start on a day that feels like a fresh start to you?
3. **Tweak your environment.** Can you make a small change to your environment to make the habit a little easier?
4. **Decide on an action trigger.** Can you decide ahead of time when you'll execute on the habit to pre-load the decision?
5. **Give yourself a cue.** Can you set up a visual cue to remind yourself of the habit when you're most likely to forget it?
6. **Form a supporting habit.** Can you start a supporting habit that will get you 20 seconds closer to your main goal?
7. **Rely on a checklist.** Can you create a checklist to help you stick to your plan?
8. **Lean on your community.** Can you invite your family, your friends, or the Facebook community for this book to support you in your goals?

6

Break the Bad Habits

I n Section 3, you'll come across a couple habits that may be getting in the way of your goal to find more happiness as a parent. (For example, in Chapter 12 you'll learn about something we all do because we think it helps our mood, but it's actually hurting our happiness.)

Most of the tools in your new habit toolbox will also help you break a bad habit. For example:

1. **Take advantage of the fresh start effect.** This works for bad habits.
2. **Give yourself a cue.** Visual cues can remind you to avoid the bad habit when you're most likely to slip back into it.
3. **Lean on your community.** Inviting your community to support you in breaking a bad habit can be just as useful as asking for support in forming a new habit.

However, breaking a bad habit does offer a unique challenge. Here are four more tools for your toolbox.

I have a few family members and friends who are trying to cut out diet soda, so I've used that example throughout this chapter. But you can apply this advice to any of your habits that need a good kick in the pants, whether it's a habit that's standing in the way of your happiness as a parent or something you've been wanting to cut out for a long time, from biting your nails to watching too much reality TV.

Remove the Temptation
You may recognize this from the last chapter because this is a form of tweaking your environment. But it's important enough to rehash from the perspective of a bad habit.

The key in tweaking your environment to break a bad habit is to remove the temptation.

For example, get all the diet soda out of your house. If you always have a soda in the morning because you're tired from staying up late, try moving your bedtime up half an hour at a time until you no longer need the caffeine or sugar to keep you going in the morning. If you always have a Diet Coke when you eat out, make a list of restaurants that serve only Pepsi products and stick to those restaurants for a while.

Think about when and where you indulge, and remove the badness (and yourself) from those situations. Get the junk food out of your pantry. Cancel your cable. Have your fingernails surgically removed.

Avoid the Void

It's easier to give up something you enjoy if you have something else enjoyable ready to take its place right away. For example, you could replace soda with:

- Lightly sweetened iced tea
- Spritzer with carbonated water and a little juice
- Iced tea mixed with a little bit of lemonade or pink lemonade

This trick was the key to my success when I kicked my own soda habit. I replaced soda with sweet iced tea, then downgraded to lightly sweetened iced tea, then unsweetened. At which point I magically lost five pounds.

Say "If...Then"

Come up with a simple "if...then" plan. For example: "If I think about ordering a soda, then I'll order an iced tea instead." Or: "If I'm at the grocery store, then I won't even walk down the soda aisle."

This is a great way to pre-load a better decision for yourself so you don't end up relying on your limited willpower.

In one study, people trying to eat less of a certain food repeated their "if...then" plan to themselves three times, and the plan helped them achieve their goal compared to people without an "if...then" plan.

Writing down your plan helps too. Try a visual cue by using washable window markers to write it on your bathroom mirror.

Look on the Bright Side

Look for the "bright spots." Are there times when it's easier than others to not indulge in your bad habit? Focus on what makes those times successful, then try to recreate those circumstances.

For example, maybe you notice that if you have a full glass of water in the morning, you aren't as tempted by a soda at lunch. Then all you have to do is drink that glass of water every morning to avoid temptation.

Your Bad Habit Toolkit

1. **Remove the temptation.** Can you make a small change to your environment to avoid the temptation of falling back into your bad habit?
2. **Avoid the void.** Can you replace the bad habit with something you'll enjoy?
3. **Say "if...then."** Pre-load a decision about how you'll avoid the bad habit.
4. **Look on the bright side.** Can you recreate the circumstances of the "bright spots" when you don't indulge in the bad habit?

7

What You Need to Know About "Me Time"

P arents need recess, too. You probably already know this. What you may *not* know is that most parents get "me time" in a way that hurts – not helps – their happiness.

First, a quick reminder: All the tasks and decisions you make throughout the day wear on your brain. This is why your brain needs regular breaks. Breaks give your brain a chance to recuperate so you don't get burned out or unleash your anger like a cranky bear.

I learned all this early on in my research after the Day I Broke. It suddenly made total sense why I'd reached my breaking point. Because I didn't have a *single* thing in my day that was just for me.

No hobbies, no alone time. My life was *all* work and kid-wrangling.

Oh, But the Guilt

When I wasn't being productive, I felt guilty. So guilty.

For that reason, I spent all my leisure time on working or keeping the house running. But the fact that I never gave myself a break is exactly why I couldn't find happiness as a parent. My brain didn't stand a chance.

By putting myself last on the never-ending to-do list, I was actually hurting my kids and my husband.

And so like a good little student of happiness, I started making time for myself during the day, every day. Something simple I could pick up and do anytime. Something free.

I started playing a game app on my tablet. The game in particular was a version of SimCity where you build your own city, complete with factories and water towers and parks. You build homes, which increase your city's population. You even have to install little sewage plants when your citizens start complaining about the plumbing situation.

Playing SimCity is a delicate balance of keeping your citizens happy, growing your population, and making sure the city's infrastructure keeps up.

I was *finally* doing something just for me. Yay me!

After about a week into this new "me time" hobby, I remember one afternoon specifically. I had managed to get the toddler and newborn to sleep at the same time, which was a rarity. Any time both little ones were asleep was my time to write and do any kind of work that required focus.

Do you know what I did instead? I played SimCity for two hours straight.

The guilt set in even *while* I was playing the game that afternoon. "What am I doing?" I thought. "I should stop!"

I didn't. I kept going. And when my husband got home from work that day, I confessed that I'd squandered all my work time on playing the stupid game.

He assured me that the break was good for me. I told myself he was right and let go of some of the guilt gnawing at me.

Something Still Didn't Feel Right

Anytime I had a few minutes free, I'd check in on the game. Build a new residence, manufacture a few donuts at the donut shop to make some money, upgrade a police station to a police precinct.

It's like my brain never stopped thinking about the game. You always had two or three different goals for what you wanted to get done in your city, and when you got them done, more goals would crop up to replace the old ones.

The game does a fantastic job of sucking you in and keeping you coming back. But instead of relaxing me, the game was giving me one more thing to worry about.

I decided to research the answer to this question: "What is the *best* way to spend your leisure time?"

What I found surprised me. I always thought that watching television and playing video games were the perfect brain break. But science shows that TV and video games do *not* make you happy.

When we have leisure time, we tend to do what's easy and convenient. We fall into old habits that don't actually add to our happiness.

That's why my first attempt at making "me time" that summer was an epic failure. Instead of recharging my batteries, the mindless game was adding to my stress.

How to Spend Leisure Time

As I learned the hard way, what you do during your "me time" matters. For example, binge-watching your favorite TV show on Netflix doesn't really help your brain recuperate from the stresses of the day.

In addition to watching TV or playing video games, here are a few more examples of what *not* to do: shopping, drinking or eating, or browsing the Internet. So what *should* you do during your leisure time?

- Spend time with friends and family – but Facebook doesn't count. You could set up a regular weekly time to get together with friends or carve out time on the weekends to just be with your family instead of doing housework or running errands.
- Do something physical, whether that's exercise or playing a sport. (Check out Chapter 15 for the full scoop on how this impacts your happiness.)
- Read a book.
- Listen to music.

These are all fantastic ways to spend your leisure time, but I haven't given you the best one of all.

The Best Kind of "Me Time"

Every day, you should be exercising your "signature strengths."

Your signature strengths are the things that you are the absolute best at compared to everything else you do. These strengths set you apart from others. When you're using your signature strength, you should feel energized. And when you're done, you should feel excited for the next time you get to do it.

What's great about finding a way to use your signature strengths every day is that the more you use them, the happier you become and the less stressed you are.

For example, I consider writing one of my signature strengths. It also happens to be my job, which is a bonus. But that means to use my signature strength in my leisure time, I need to write something just for me.

Your signature strength might be completely different from mine. A few examples for you:

- Making things with your own two hands, from knitting to woodworking
- Coming up with new recipes
- Learning something new, such as reading a nonfiction book or following your curiosity on Wikipedia
- Volunteering
- Doing crossword puzzles
- Sketching or making art
- Working with numbers, such as balancing the checkbook or doing financial planning for your family

Do It Now

1. Grab a pen and paper.
2. Set a timer for 10 minutes.
3. Ask yourself: "What are my signature strengths?" Write down everything that comes to mind, even if you're not 100 percent sure.
4. When the timer's up, go back through your list and for each idea, ask these questions:
   - Does this bring me joy?
   - When I'm doing it, do I feel energized?
   - When I'm done with it, do I look forward to when I can do it again?
5. For every idea where you answered "yes" to all three questions, circle it. Those are your signature strengths.

Now that you know your signature strengths, find a way to use them every day. Use the new habit toolbox in Chapter 5 to make sure your new strength habit will stick.

And if you feel guilty for spending time on doing something you love, remember that your brain needs a break from the daily slog of chauffeuring kids and making well-balanced meals and doing laundry.

Your family will reap the benefits of a happier you.

Section 3
Tinker to Find Your Recipe

8

Reflect

One of the best rituals you can incorporate to bring more happiness to your life? Reflecting on what you're grateful for.

Why Gratitude Works Like Magic

A gratitude ritual makes your brain happy by boosting the neurotransmitters dopamine and serotonin. What's more, research shows that people with a gratitude ritual cope better with everyday stress. Everyday stress is pretty much synonymous with parenting life, so gratitude is the perfect happiness habit for you.

But you won't get these benefits if you focus on gratitude just once in a while. The effects will wear off, and you'll start taking things for granted again. You must make gratitude part of your routine. Once a week is the bare minimum. In my family, we go around the table at dinnertime to share what everyone is grateful for – *even* the toddler.

And here's a funny tidbit for you: As it turns out, it doesn't even matter if you can't think of something you're grateful for. I'm embarrassed to admit it, but this happens to me all the time.

For example, let's say the toddler is throwing a tantrum because she wants a snack five minutes before dinner's ready, the baby spit up all over me, and the dog just walked into the kitchen smacking her lips after a visit to the cats' litter box.

Instead of screaming and running from the house, I try to catch myself in those moments and ask: "What am I grateful for?"

If I can't think of anything in that moment, it's okay. I *still* get the benefits of a gratitude habit. Not only that, by continuing to ask myself that question, I'm making it easier to answer myself the next time.

This is because remembering to be grateful affects the neuron density in the prefrontal cortex of your brain, making the neurons more efficient. And that's a very good thing because it's the prefrontal cortex that acts as the "grown-up" and keeps you from playing video games all day or reacting like a three-year-old to every minor disappointment.

You *want* your prefrontal cortex to be nice and efficient because it's the part of your brain that keeps you working toward long-term goals. This is the part of your brain that helps you decide to do the right thing. It's the part of your brain that keeps you from unleashing epic vengeance after your teenager borrows your favorite sweater and accidentally squirts ketchup on it.

A happy, healthy prefrontal cortex means a happy, healthy you.

How to Do It

Here are a few ideas for gratitude rituals:

- Go around the table at dinnertime and ask, "What are you grateful for?" If dinner isn't a good fit for your family, try another meal or a time when you're all together every day. The benefit of doing the ritual with your family is they get the happiness boost as well.

- Keep a gratitude journal for yourself. Reflect on your gratitude by writing in your journal once a day. I personally use a journaling app on my phone to record my gratitudes, which I link to at the end of this chapter. Sometimes I also add a picture to my daily entry.

- Post a family gratitude list. Hang a big piece of posterboard and invite your family members to add a sticky note whenever they think of something they're grateful for. An alternative approach is to put a jar somewhere central in your house and ask your family to write gratitudes on a slip of paper to put in the jar. Then at the end of every week – and maybe again on the last day of the year – you can read through the gratitudes together.

- Start every day with thanks. Text someone you know a quick message of appreciation, or send an email to share why you're grateful for them. Write a note to slip into your child's lunch to share what you appreciate about them.

3 Gratitude Gotchas

Keep these points in mind as you start a gratitude ritual:

- Whichever ritual you choose, you'll get the greatest benefit by reflecting on *unique* gratitudes every time. For example, if you say the same thing every night at the dinner table, you'll be going through the motions and not feel the full effects of the gratitude. Challenge yourself (and your family) to come up with something new every time.

- What you're grateful for doesn't have to be huge like, "I'm grateful for my healthy family." Sometimes those big gratitudes can be too intangible for you to fully feel the gratitude. You can be grateful for getting a rockstar parking spot in the front row at the grocery store, for finding a piece of leftover Halloween candy at the back of the pantry, or for finally getting to the bottom of the laundry hamper.

- If you encounter a situation where you struggle to come up with something you're grateful for, no worries. Try these tricks:
  - Imagine *not* having something you love. This might sound morbid, but it works. For example, imagine if your child had not been born or if your partner was suddenly absent from your life. What would your life look like?
  - Give up something you love for a few days. I guarantee after seven days without coffee or chocolate, you'll be grateful for those simple pleasures.

Supplies You'll Need

Depending on how you decide to fit in a gratitude ritual, you might want some of these:

- A gratitude journal or a journaling app for your phone. You'll find a few options I love at idealistmom.com/happy-you-resources.
- For a family gratitude list, you'll want a piece of posterboard and sticky notes or a jar with slips of paper nearby.

9

Cut the Clutter

Everyone has different triggers for anger. For some people, it's dishes in the sink, or kids whining, or stepping on a LEGO. My number one trigger? Feeling overwhelmed.

When my head swirls with bills to pay, housework, errands, freelance deadlines – and then I'm running late getting out of the house to get to an appointment and my toddler won't let me brush her teeth – I overreact *majorly*.

But Here's the Worst Part

On a normal day, toddler defiance over tooth-brushing doesn't push me over the edge. But when I have underlying stress about work, finances, and keeping the house in order, my inner grizzly bear comes out to play.

And she doesn't play nice. When I lose my cool, my 2-year-old reacts by hanging her head. She won't make eye contact with me, and it breaks my heart.

Research shows that for every one of these negative interactions, you need five positive interactions to rebuild the relationship. That's a whole lot of *Goodnight Moon*, and I'm not sure I'm up for it.

A Better Way

When I feel the pressure of my to-do list start to build, my tone with my kids gets short and snappy.

This is my warning sign. My clue that if I don't do something soon, I could blow up at these little people who look to me for love, guidance, and snacks.

Lately, I've been doing something new when those warning bells go off. If you tend to feel stressed, overwhelmed, or unorganized, this trick will probably help you, too.

The Problem With Your Brain

The short-term memory part of your brain is similar to the RAM of your computer. When you have 20 different applications open, the computer will likely act sluggish because that's more than it can handle at one time.

Your short-term memory is the same way. You can successfully hold two or three items in your mind at once, but anything beyond that will make you feel distracted and overwhelmed by your own mental load.

Translation? A swirling cloud of "should"s in your head sets you up to lose your temper with your kids.

An easy way to combat this is to come up with a single place where you write *everything* down. This is the master list you set up in Chapter 3. But I did that already, so why was I still a ticking time bomb with my kids?

The Simple – And Not So Simple – Answer

Bills and unsorted mail on my kitchen counter. Notes from my 7-year-old's school on the fridge. A mountain of laundry teetering precariously on top of the dryer. A 100-page draft to edit for a client, sitting on the dining room table.

Each area where the stuff piles up represents several more things I should be doing.

All this clutter distracts me. Weighs on me. Makes me agitated. Research shows this isn't just in my head. Clutter really does mess with your brain and increase your stress.

But when is a busy mom supposed to find time to sit down and organize the whole house when she's already feeling overwhelmed?

4 Steps to Reset Your Brain

When my agitation level starts to ramp up, this is what I do:

1. Pick one cluttered surface in your house or at work. It could be the kitchen counter, your desk, or that chair. (You know the one. I'm convinced every house has *that* chair where the laundry and jackets and toys pile up.)
2. Set a timer for 20 minutes.
3. Dump everything from that surface in a box or a laundry basket. Don't look at anything, just take one arm and sweep it across the whole surface and shove everything into the box. (p.s. This step happens to feel *awesome*, so go with gusto.)
4. For the next 20 minutes, go through that box, one item at a time, sorting into categories:
   o Trash/recycle
   o To file
   o To put away
   o To add to your master list

Don't start putting stuff away during your 20 minutes. You can do that later. Stay put in one place and tackle that clutter before it tackles you.

When the timer's up, put each pile where it belongs. If you're short on time, the "to file" pile can go on top of your filing cabinet. The "master list" pile can go on top of your planner or laptop or wherever you keep your list. Even the "to put away" pile can be deposited outside the door of whichever room the item belongs in.

If you didn't get through the box in 20 minutes, save it for another time and set your timer again.

The key: Make a dent in the clutter that's overloading your senses, so you can reset your brain and be ready to tackle whatever the day brings – whether that's toddler tooth-brushing or a big presentation to your boss, or both.

10

Enjoy a Childhood Pastime

C an I admit something? Sometimes it feels *good* to be in a bad mood. You get to stomp around the house, ranting about toy clutter and overreacting to your toddler spilling her juice on the kitchen floor. Everyone knows to stay out of your way, and you can feel good about the fact that you're right and everyone else is wrong.

Like *real* good. To me, it almost feels like my brain is riding the high of a bad mood.

I learned recently that my rudimentary understanding isn't far off from the truth.

This Is Your Brain in a Bad Mood

When you're already stressed, your brain – or more specifically, the amygdala of your brain – becomes hyper-vigilant. Your brain interprets even the smallest of everyday annoyances as a threat against your survival. That's the amygdala (uh-mig-duh-luh) at work.

For example, let's say something happened to put you in a bad mood. Then you realize your toddler made a mess in her diaper and you need to stop what you're doing to change it.

And you *lose* it. Not because changing a diaper is a ridiculous expectation of a parent, but because your brain is shut down to logic and interpreting every little thing as a threat.

The creepy part is that you can actually become addicted to the cocktail of stress hormones your body releases to cope when you lose your temper.

When the stress kicks in, you get a nice rush of adrenaline. And when you finally resolve the bad mood, endorphins kick in. The bigger the stress ball you were, the bigger the dose of endorphins you get when all is said and done.

So when I relish my day-long bad mood? I'm basically a junkie looking for my next biggest fix.

But That's Not the Worst Part

Constant stress isn't just impacting your happiness or your family's happiness.

Research shows that chronic stress actually shrinks the size of your brain's hippocampus. This little doohickey is integral to forming memories, so it's kind of an important part of the brain that you will probably want to keep as healthy as possible. I mean, if you can't find your keys now, just imagine what it will be like after a lifetime of unnecessary stress shrinking your brain.

An Easy Way to Get Your Brain Back on Track

Remember how the amygdala of your brain goes into overreact-to-everything mode? Those little almond-shaped clusters at the base of your brain act as a gateway to the whole process of stress hormones and a shrinking brain and everything you *don't* want.

Closing the gateway will be the key for turning your bad mood around.

And here's how: When you feel a horrible, no-good, very bad mood threatening to ruin your day, grab one of your kid's coloring books, and start coloring.

That may sound a little crazy, but it works. The action of coloring calls on both logic (staying in the lines) and creativity (picking colors and color schemes), and that combo package is exactly what your amygdala needs to chill out.

When you color, you lower the activity of the amygdala and encourage your mind to focus – something that just isn't possible when you're on the rampage.

By forcing yourself to focus, you make it impossible for your brain to sustain that rampage.

So go ahead and color. You can color Disney characters or a mandala pattern or a coloring book for hipsters. It doesn't matter.

Just hole up with your coloring book of choice, some good old-fashioned crayons, and go to town while your brain relaxes.

Supplies You'll Need

- A coloring book or a free coloring page, which you can download from lots of places.
- Crayons or high-quality coloring pencils or markers. Side note: My mother-in-law asked for a coloring book and markers for Christmas, and one of her sons thought it would be funny to give her a dollar store coloring book and kids' markers. Not quite the same calming effect, as it turns out.
- Check out all my favorites at idealistmom.com/happy-you-resources.

11

Hug It Out

I am not what you would call a "hugger." Sure, I hug my close friends and family. But acquaintances and co-workers? Those hugs feel forced and awkward, and it's like my body has forgotten how to execute on a hug.

Which side do I tilt my head to? Do I use both arms? What if I use only one arm, but it's the same side arm they use, and our arms meet in the middle in a clumsy hug-and-high-five hybrid?

Clearly, I am in need of some coaching in the casual hugging department. But not too long ago, I learned it wasn't just the casual hugs I was struggling with.

The way I was hugging my husband and kids was all wrong.

Here's Why

To get the happy chemicals oxytocin and serotonin flowing, you need to hold a hug for at least *six seconds*.

Why is that important? Those are the chemicals that boost your mood and promote bonding. In particular, oxytocin reduces the reactivity of the amygdala.

If you've already read Chapter 10 on coloring, you've learned that when you're stressed, the amygdala of your brain becomes hyper-vigilant. Suddenly, you interpret even the smallest of everyday annoyances as a threat against your survival. That's the work of the amygdala (uh-mig-duh-luh).

For example, let's say something happened to put you in a bad mood – a tantrum from your toddler, realizing you missed a bill due date and now owe a $50 late fee, or finally finishing the mountain of laundry only to discover piles and piles shoved under your kid's bed. Then your 7-year-old walks up and says, "I'm hungry."

And you lose it. Not because your child had a ridiculous request, but because your brain is shut down to logic and interpreting every little thing as a threat.

To find happiness as a parent, you need your amygdala to chill out. And oxytocin is how you do that.

But Hugging...*Really?*

After I learned this, I paid attention to the hugs I gave my husband and kids for a couple days. I counted to myself while we hugged.

Three seconds here, half a second there. Our hugs – if we remembered to exchange them – were rushed.

After a couple days of those quick, bland hugs, I decided to do my own experiment. When my husband got home from work, I walked up to him and opened my arms for a hug. Then instead of letting go after a couple seconds, I just kept hugging.

And the funniest thing happened.

After six seconds, my body felt warmer.

Eight seconds, and my body relaxed into his.

Ten seconds, I let go of a deep breath I didn't realize I'd been holding.

After our crazy busy day filled with work drama and toddler temper tantrums, we just...connected.

Everything else *melted away.*

That hug recharged me so I could face whatever came my way – from picky eating at dinner to epic bedtime stalling.

The Magic Number of Hugs

Not only does length matter when it comes to hugs, but how many times you hug matters to your happiness.

Research shows that to get the full benefit of the happy chemicals created by hugs, you need eight hugs a day.

Eight hugs a day of six seconds or more adds up to 48 seconds. In other words, in less than a minute a day you can change the chemical make-up of your body so you end up happier.

Take the Hugging Challenge

Here's how:

1. Promise yourself to give **8 hugs today** – to your partner, your kids, or anyone else you feel comfortable giving a good quality hug. Maybe skip your boss for this exercise.
2. Say it out loud to make the commitment official: "I will give 8 hugs today."
3. For every hug, make sure it lasts 6 seconds or more. Count in your head if you have to.
4. Print the bonus scorecard included with this book to keep track of your hugs and mark off one box for every awesome hug you deliver. You could even recruit your family to join you in the challenge too and print off one scorecard per person. Keep your scorecard somewhere handy but visible, like on the fridge, next to your phone, or taped to your steering wheel. (By the way, this is a visual cue to help you form the habit. Refer to Chapter 5 for more about visual cues.)

12

The One Habit Everyone Should Break

Being home all day with my kids is a blessing. I know that, and I appreciate it. But that doesn't change the fact that I'm home all day with my *kids*.

Recently, I was nursing my newborn girl Charlie on the living room couch when I realized my toddler was awful quiet.

I heard a rustle in the dining room, so while still nursing, I awkwardly pushed off the couch to have a look.

And when I rounded the corner, I chuckled at myself. Because Bailey was just sitting at the kids' art table, scribbling away.

"Are you drawing, honey?" I asked.

She stopped and stared at me. "Yeah," she said.

I turned to head back to the living room, shaking my head and feeling silly for worrying.

But Wait...

Why did she stop what she was doing?

I whipped back around and hurried to where Bailey was sitting. In her hand?

A blue Sharpie.

On the art table. The nice dining room chair. Her arms. Her belly. All over her hands. HER FACE.

She looked up at me, and she suddenly got very, very still. Which is saying something for her.

So yes, I'm lucky to be home with my kids. But that doesn't mean my first reaction was to skip off, tra-la-la-ing to retrieve the rubbing alcohol. (Which, in case you find yourself in a similar situation one day, worked on the toddler's skin but *not* the wood table or chair. I've since learned that toothpaste will do the trick, though.)

After I scrubbed her arms and hands and belly and face until she resembled a sunburned Strawberry Shortcake, I went to rescue baby Charlie from the bouncy seat on the bathroom counter.

And I guess she must've been feeling left out of all the fun we were having.

When I lifted her out of her seat, a glob of mustard yellow dropped to the counter. I held her away from my body and peered around to her back. An impressive out-the-back-and-both-leg-holes variety of blowout.

So yes, I feel immense gratitude for my life. But that doesn't mean I laid the baby gently on the changing table, then fist-pumped the air in anticipation of the awesome task ahead.

After I changed the baby's diaper and wiped her down and cleaned the bathroom counter and got her dressed again, it dawned on me that I hadn't seen Bailey in a while.

I walked out of the bathroom into the bedroom and saw her standing on the arm of the rocking chair. All the better to reach into the top drawer of the dresser.

And I started walking faster because I realized what we keep in that top drawer of the dresser.

As I got closer, I saw the wrappers on the floor under the open dresser drawer.

"Oh, God," I said.

Condoms.

She'd unwrapped every single one and let the wrappers fall. And in her hands?

The things themselves. All clumped together in her innocent little hands.

So yes, I'm happy for the gift of seeing my girls all day every day. But that doesn't mean I cheerfully hummed a Mary Poppins tune as I pried the clump from her hands and held her up to the bathroom sink where I washed her hands for 27 minutes.

What You Might Not Expect

This all happened before 10 am.

I did not text my husband a play-by-play of the morning.

I did not call him to share a laundry list of grievances.

I did not take a photo of each epic mess and send it to him.

Why? Because there's *nothing* he could do to help. It's not like he can reach through the phone to scrub permanent marker, baby poo, and condom slime.

Venting does nothing to dissolve anger. All venting does is intensify my anger to the boiling point.

And he can't leave work on a moment's notice to come home and stay with the kids so I can lock myself in the upstairs bathroom with a bag of Dove chocolate and a box of wine. (Yes, we're classy boxed wine folk.)

Here's What Complaining Does Accomplish

Complaining about every little (or big) hiccup gives me a skewed perspective of my day. Complaining puts my focus squarely on the problem. *Not* the solution.

And when you complain, your brain releases stress hormones that get in the way of your ability to think clearly.

The crazy part is that even if you're just listening to someone else complain, your brain also releases stress hormones. Not only was complaining to my husband Ty stressing *him* out, but it also made him feel powerless.

His wife is about to throw Tickle Me Elmo off a cliff, and he can't do a thing to help her.

Ty never actually told me all this. But I know.

I know because after Bailey was born and I still had a desk job, Ty stayed home with Bailey one afternoon a week.

On those afternoons, I peppered him with questions. *Is she napping okay? Did she take the bottle I left? Is she being fussy? Is he getting any work done?*

And of course, as is the case when you try to get work done while watching kids, the answers were usually: *No, no, yes, no.*

I wanted to help. But I was stuck at work. And my husband at home with a fussy, non-sleeping baby was all I could think about, so I wasn't even being super productive at work.

I Made a Pact With Myself

When I left my corporate job to become a full-time blogger – as "full-time" as you can be while wrangling a toddler and a newborn – I vowed not to complain to my husband about all the little bumps in the road. I needed to stop complaining in order to be a happy mom.

It took me a while to tell him about my pact, and when I did, he wasn't actually a fan of it.

He wants me to tell him about those everyday frustrations. He wants to know if I'm on the brink of moving to Canada to start a new life as a Mountie.

So I promised if I'm really at my breaking point, I will tell him. And he will get away from work if he can and come give me a break.

For everything else, I don't text. I don't call.

If I happen to feel a burning desire to share a frustrating story before I see him in person, I try to focus on a solution, *not* the problem. Or I wait until I can laugh about it.

Complaining in the moment doesn't do anyone any good. And it definitely doesn't make me a happy mother.

Happy Parents Don't Do This Either

The moment my husband walks through the door after work, I can barely contain myself.

I'm ready to unload all the crappy parts of my day. But *again*, I hold back.

When I haven't seen my husband all day, the last thing I want to do is get all worked up into a froth of anger as my first interaction with him.

And the same goes for him. We both avoid unloading our frustrations first thing when we see each other. Complaining right off the bat infiltrates the tone of our whole evening together.

Instead, we greet each other with a hug. And not just any kind of hug. (See Chapter 11 for more on this.)

We share the funny parts of our days, we play a quick game of chase with the kids, or we have an impromptu dance party in the kitchen. Only then do we take a deep breath and share those daily annoyances.

And here's the *best* part: After a hug and a few giggles, those frustrations transform into just another opportunity to share a laugh. Happy mom, happy family.

A Confession

On *those* days, it's hard to stop from complaining, and I'm not perfect. As my husband reminds me almost daily: Ideals are a vision, not a reality. When I slip up, I forgive myself and get my mindset back on track.

That crazy morning, I have to admit that I did text my husband.

Twice.

The first: *Do you think it's okay to use rubbing alcohol to clean the kids' art table?* I focused on the solution, not the problem. Score!

And the second: *I think Bailey's telling us she's ready for another sibling. I'll explain later.*

Take a No-Complaint Challenge

This may be the trickiest habit to break, but it's worth it. For something as ingrained as venting and complaining in our daily lives, it's important to remember that 100 percent is impossible. You will slip up from time to time. Forgive yourself and move on.

To renew my commitment to this goal, I set a no-complaint challenge for myself once in a while. I try to do it for a week or a month, once or twice a year.

Because 100 percent is impossible, the goal of this challenge is *not* to stop complaining. The goal is to raise awareness of the times you do complain so you can reframe your thoughts and words in a more positive way. Here's how you take the no-complaint challenge:

1. Pick a time period that feels doable. That could be a day, a week, or even a month.
2. Ask someone in your community to join you. This could be a friend, your partner, or someone in the *Happy You, Happy Family* Facebook community. The challenge will work best if you find someone whom you interact with every day.

3. Find a visual cue you can wear on your wrist. This could be a bracelet, a hair tie, or a rubber band. You can even use a watch, but the key is for this to be something you don't usually wear on your wrist.

4. As you go through your day if you catch yourself venting or complaining, stop and move the item on your wrist to the other wrist. Repeat this every time you notice yourself complaining.

5. If you want, you can also keep a tally of how many times you moved the bracelet or rubber band each day. Challenge yourself to lower the total every day.

What to Do Instead

As you learned in Chapter 6, it's easier to break a bad habit if you can put something else in its place.

In the words of Maya Angelou:

"What you're supposed to do when you don't like a thing is change it. If you can't change it, change the way you think about it. Don't complain."

Here are a few ideas for what to do each time you notice yourself complaining:

- **Transition from complaining about a problem to brainstorming a solution.** This is my favorite approach, and we've even started saying this mantra in my family: "We don't focus on problems. We come up with solutions."

- **Add a "but…"** When you catch yourself mid-complaint, add a "but…" and follow it up with something positive. For example, you might say, "The kids never let me focus on work." Then you could add, "But I'm grateful they want to spend time with me because when they hit the teen years, it'll be the other way around." This approach gives you a bonus happiness boost by helping you focus on the bright side and find something to be grateful for. (Refer to Chapter 8 for more on the effects of gratitude.)

- **Change "I have to" to "I get to."** I catch myself saying this all the time. "I have to leave at 2:00 to pick Abby up at school." By changing "I have to" to "I get to," you change to an appreciative tone. For example: "I *get* to leave at 2:00 to pick Abby up at school." I get to see my child at the end of the school day instead of waiting until 5:00 or 6:00 pm like I did when I had a desk job.

- **Say "Enough about that."** Sometimes it may be difficult to transition to a positive statement. In that case, stop the complaint in its tracks by giving a dismissive wave of your hand and saying "Enough about that." Then start talking about something good instead.

Supplies You'll Need

A visual cue you can wear on your wrist, such as:

- A bracelet
- A hair tie
- A rubber band

13

Hack Your Sleep

I f you're not getting enough sleep, you will *not* find happiness in the chaos of parenting life. Unless you happen to be part of the 2.5 percent of people who can thrive on less than seven hours of sleep a night, research has shown time and time again that lack of sleep will stand in the way of your daily happiness.

But I Get It

You're busy. Your kids won't let you sleep. You need some quality time just for you. Maybe all of the above.

I blame the fact that I haven't slept three hours straight in three years on my precious little ones.

1. My eldest didn't sleep through the night until she was four
2. At the age of one, my middle child went a whole month without sleeping a full night
3. I night-weaned her after the Month of No Sleep, but then the only way she'd fall asleep and stay asleep was with me lying next to her so she could wrap her little fingers up in my hair

Then last year, we reached a turning point. Finally, *finally* both big kids were sleeping through the night. Unfortunately, the turning point came while I was eight months pregnant and so I didn't get to reap the benefits.

Here Comes Baby Number Three

When my third little one was born last summer, she surprised the heck out of us by sleeping through the night at six weeks old.

I'd heard of this happening from fellow parents, but honestly I thought they were stretching the truth a bit. I didn't actually *believe* babies were capable of sleeping through the night.

From six weeks to four months old, baby Charlie slept through the night about 90 percent of the time.

And then. The four-month sleep regression.

She. Just. Wouldn't. Freaking. Sleep.

We did all the "right" things – playing white noise, sticking to a schedule so she didn't get over-tired, putting her down drowsy but awake.

Stuff that all worked when she was a couple months old. But now? Nope.

Putting her down "drowsy but awake" pissed her off majorly, signing us up for an extra 45 minutes or more to get her settled back down again.

Then she'd wake up all through the night, requiring Herculean effort from us to get her back to sleep. Even trading off between my husband and I wasn't enough to cope.

I paced the house with her at 1:00 in the morning. 2:00. 3:00. Sometimes all in a row in the same night.

I stumbled over my own feet. When my toddler woke up in the morning, I just laid on the couch and told her to pretend she's a doctor and I'm a very, very sick patient. My husband started a steady IV drip of coffee to get through every workday.

We turned into zombies.

You Can't Control Your Kids

It wasn't selfish of us to want more sleep. Lack of sleep will lower your IQ, make it harder to be happy, and even increase your risk of an early death.

You read that right. DEATH.

Zombies, indeed.

But nothing I did would get my baby to sleep more than a couple hours at a time. This served as a painful reminder of one particular secret to happiness as a parent:

You can't control your kids.

If I couldn't get my kids to sleep all night, I'd need to hack my own sleep habits so I could feel more rested.

The Answer: 20 Minutes

If you aren't already napping as a way to catch up on sleep, you should be.

But, but, but…, I can hear you thinking.

You're too busy. You can't fall asleep during the day. You have a day job.

Whatever your excuse, forget about it for now. All I'm asking you to do is try to fit in one nap once a day for the next week or so. If you're not into naps, that's okay. Just try it. If it doesn't work out for you after you give it an honest chance, then you have my permission to leave it out of your personal recipe for happiness.

Why 20 minutes? You can actually go super hardcore and train your body to get as little as two hours of sleep and still feel as well-rested as you do after eight hours. It's called polyphasic sleep, and you'll need to read a book by an expert to get the details on how to make it happen. (You'll find the link at the end of this chapter.)

But the simplest and most realistic approach to polyphasic sleep is to add one 20-minute nap during the day. When you do this, your overnight sleep needs bump down to just six hours of sleep.

How to Make Naps Happen

Ready to give naps a chance? Keep these tidbits in mind:

- Even five minutes can help. And who doesn't have five minutes? The brain boost that you get from a nap even outperforms the effects of caffeine.
- If you're home during the day, you can grab a power nap while your kid naps or even set an older kid up to play independently while you catch some zzz's.

- If you work outside the home, nap in your car during your lunch break or in between meetings. A short nap can make you more productive and alert, so don't feel bad about taking a quick break. And hey, it's a lot healthier than taking a smoke break or hitting up the vending machines. This is why pilots, air traffic controllers, and nurses grab power naps while on the job.

- The optimal length of time for a nap depends on what effect you're going for. For a quick boost in energy and focus, 25 minutes or less is best. But if you nap somewhere between 30 minutes and 85 minutes, you'll likely wake up pretty groggy. For a deeper sleep, set your alarm for 90 minutes because that's a full sleep cycle.

- If you want to try a power nap but you're worried you'll sleep through an alarm, I have an easy fix for you. Drink coffee right before you lay down. The caffeine will take about 20 minutes to kick in, so you'll wake up feeling refreshed *with* an extra jolt from the caffeine.

Supplies You'll Need

For all the details on how to do polyphasic sleep the right way, visit idealistmom.com/happy-you-resources.

14

Just Stop

I didn't name this chapter what it *should* be named because I was worried you'd pass it up. But this daily habit is one of the absolute best things you can do to reach your goal of more happiness as a parent.

The real reason I was worried you'd skip this chapter is because before I wrote this book, I would have skipped it. In my research, over and over again this suggestion popped up. And every time, I ignored it.

I pictured some childless woman decked out head to toe in trendy athleisure-wear (ironed, of course), sitting cross-legged on the floor with her back straight as a board, perfectly manicured hands facing palms up, dainty wrists resting on her knees. Saying "om" and relishing the complete and utter peace without screaming children, barking dogs, or the alarm bell of an off-kilter washing machine to distract her.

From my perspective, it was impossible for meditating and parenting to exist together in the same house.

A Turning Point

But after the Day I Broke, I invited my family to support me in my goal to find more happiness as a parent. I asked my toddler to remind me to calm down if she noticed me getting frustrated. And I asked my husband for help.

He joined me in my happiness research, and it didn't take him long to happen upon the science behind meditation and how it leads to greater happiness. The same science I'd skipped over again and again.

"We should try meditating," he said.

"Ugh," I said.

"No, it'll be good. We'll both do it."

"Ugh."

Clearly, I'm a pleasant person to spend your days with.

But he persisted and did the research to find a high-quality phone app to guide our meditation. He tested it himself first, then took the baby from my arms, handed me his phone and a pair of noise-canceling headphones, and shooed me off to the bedroom.

"Do I *have* to?"

"Just 10 minutes," he said.

He shut the door behind me, and I sighed.

I settled onto the floor, plopped the headphones on, and started the app. And boy, did I *not* want to be wasting 10 minutes on that.

The app directed me to focus on my breath. Which sounds easy, but when you're a grown woman pouting over a 10-minute task that's actually good for you, it's surprisingly difficult to focus on just your breath.

Still, I did it.

And the funniest thing happened.

This may be a little too much information, but it's the proof that convinced me to make meditation a daily habit, even after all my huffing and puffing about it.

First, you should understand that I'm still nursing my baby.

Now here's the kicker: After about five minutes of focusing on my breath, my milk let down.

I couldn't hear my baby. She wasn't anywhere near me. I wasn't even thinking about her.

But meditating relaxed me so thoroughly and completely that *my milk let down*.

That may be more than you wanted to know, but my body's physiological response to meditating is what convinced me. More than reading all the science behind why it's so good for you.

I still grumbled to myself during the whole 10 minutes, but I couldn't deny my body's own reaction. Plus, I've found that it doesn't matter how you feel *during* meditation. It's how you feel after that counts.

When my 10 minutes was over, I opened my eyes and felt an immense sense of peace. A peace I've never felt before in my life.

And so I was hooked. (But I still won't be ironing my yoga pants.)

Why Meditation Is So Good for You

Meditation isn't just some nice-to-have daily habit. It actually changes your brain over time.

For example, let's say your toddler found a Sharpie and went to town decorating your recently refinished hardwood floors.

When you have a daily meditation habit, your brain is less likely to interpret an upsetting event like that as a threat. Your brain is more capable of looking at the situation from a rational perspective. And the parts of your brain that control empathy get stronger.

Now, maybe you don't *want* to feel empathy for your mischievous toddler, but the benefits of meditation are exactly what your brain needs to protect you from the chaos of parenting life.

You'll be less likely to blow up at your kids, you'll experience less stress, and you'll be happier. Win-win-win.

Yes, Even Parents Can Meditate

A few helpful tips on meditating, from one parent to another:

- Any little bit helps. If all you can afford is two minutes, you'll still see benefits. And I *know*. I do. You have the dishes and the bills and the call of Netflix. But the small amount of time you give up will repay you many times over.

- You can meditate anywhere comfortable. Sitting on the floor or in a chair, lying down, or even waiting in your car in the school pickup line.

- I use an app on my phone and noise-canceling headphones to drown out the kids' shenanigans. Click the links at the end of this chapter for details on what I use.

- Consider trading kid duty with your partner so you can both get the benefits of meditation. Pick an action trigger like when everyone gets home at the end of the day. For example, "When we get home from work, I'll pass the baby to my husband and shut myself up in the bedroom to meditate."

Get the Kids Involved

You can even start a meditation habit that includes the whole family. This makes for a great bedtime ritual with your kids.

One effective way to meditate with kids is to practice loving-kindness meditation. This may sound a little weird, but the science shows that practicing this particular style of meditation leads to more happiness.

All you do for this meditation is repeat a series of phrases directed at different people each time. The most common phrases are some variation of these:

May you be safe.
May you be healthy.
May you be happy.
May you be peaceful and at ease.

But you can make the phrases whatever you'd like. Feel free to ask your kids what they'd like to say because you'll be saying it together every day.

After you decide on the phrases you'll use, this is how you go through the loving-kindness meditation:

1. Speak the phrases directed at yourself: "May I be safe. May I be healthy. May I be happy. May I be peaceful and at ease."
2. Speak the phrases again but directed at someone you feel thankful for or someone who has helped you. Picture the person's face and say: "May you be safe. May you be healthy. May you be happy. May you be peaceful and at ease."
3. This time, visualize someone you feel neutral about – someone you neither like or dislike. Speak the phrases directed at that person.
4. Finally, visualize someone you don't like or someone you're having a hard time with. For kids, this might be a teacher they're clashing with or another kid who's teasing or bullying them. Speak the phrases one last time directed at that person.

Supplies You'll Need

- An app to guide you, especially if you've never tried meditating before. I tried a bunch of different apps, and you'll find my favorite app at idealistmom.com/happy-you-resources.
- Even if my husband's on kid duty, I find that I still need noise-canceling headphones to maintain my focus. My favorites are listed at idealistmom.com/happy-you-resources.

15

Shake It Up

You won't find a chapter in this book called "Exercise Every Day." Even though a regular exercise habit is one of the best things you can do to live a happier life, I couldn't bring myself to write that chapter.

The main reason? I don't have a regular exercise habit myself, so I'd be a hypocrite if I told you that *you* had to exercise every day.

The truth is that every time I hit a groove on the exercise front, something gets in the way like vacation or sickness or wanting to sit on my butt.

What You Should Know About Exercise And Happiness

Before we get to the happiness habit that I wholeheartedly recommend based on my research *and* experience, you should know that the impact of exercise on your brain is undeniable.

You've probably already heard that exercise boosts your endorphins, which is a chemical that helps you fight stress. Exercise also prompts your body to release a special protein called BDNF, which stands for Brain-Derived Neurotrophic Factor. This protein is like a reset switch for your brain, so you typically feel at ease and happier after exercising. And after an angry outburst, physical activity helps flush the adrenaline from your system.

If you do want to establish an exercise habit, here are a few things to help you find success:

- Use the habit-forming tools from Chapter 5. The only time I've had success sticking to a regular exercise routine is when I created a plan up front using those habit tricks.
- Here's a brilliant supporting habit that might work for you: When you go to bed, put your workout clothes on top of your alarm clock or your phone.
- All you need is **20 minutes** of physical activity to get a happiness boost. The first 20 minutes of exercise will give you most of the health benefits and the biggest improvement to your mood. Anything beyond that is gravy. That's 20 minutes a day, though. If you skip a day of exercise, your mood won't get the boost on that day. This is useful to know because if you have one day a week that you usually struggle more than others, you know to prioritize exercising on that day. For example, if Mondays are always stressful as you get back into the weekly routine of work and school, you might want to start a habit of walking for 20 minutes at lunch every Monday to keep yourself on track.
- But with that said, you should start small to increase your chances of success. The first week, start with just five minutes. You can walk around the block, walk up and down the stairs inside your house or outside your apartment building, or do jumping jacks. Then the next week, add a minute. Keep going until you get to 20 minutes a day.

As I write, I'm in the middle of re-establishing an exercise habit that went by the wayside during a family vacation. Here's my plan to show you how your habit toolbox can work together:

1. **Tweak your environment.** At all times, we leave a yoga DVD queued up in the DVD player.
2. **Decide on an action trigger.** When my husband gets home from work, I hand over the baby and start the yoga DVD.

3. **Form a supporting habit.** When I get home from picking my eldest daughter from school, I immediately change into a t-shirt and comfy yoga pants.

4. **Lean on your community.** I got my husband on board with wrangling the baby, then I invited my toddler and big kid to join in on the yoga DVD with me.

Now, Back to the Point of This Chapter

As much as I grouse about exercising regularly, I have found one way to increase my daily physical activity that's actually fun for me *and* my kids.

A family dance party.

Research shows that upbeat music cuts your stress, for example by reducing levels of the stress hormone cortisol. What's more, babies and toddlers get a big dose of happy when moving their bodies to a rhythmic beat.

Next time you and/or your kids feel a case of the crankies coming on, fire up your favorite playlist and dance away the bad mojo.

You'll tire the kids out before bedtime, plus you'll burn a few calories yourself. Which means you can skip working out, or at least skip feeling guilty for not working out. You're welcome!

What You Need for a Successful Dance Party

A few tips to keep in mind:

- Use a playlist that's fun for the *whole family* to shake their booties to. Check the supplies list at the end of this chapter for my favorite dance party playlists. My playlists are made up of contemporary, upbeat tunes with clean language but aren't so kiddish that you'll lock yourself in the bathroom until they're over. No Yo Gabba Gabba, I promise.

- Don't consider yourself a good dancer? Yeah, me neither. Just be silly and move your body. As a side benefit, the sillier you are, the more you'll laugh. Laughter lowers your levels of stress hormones and releases endorphins.

- Family dance parties work especially well with action triggers. For example, you might decide to have a daily dance party after school before the kids start homework.

Supplies You'll Need

For a few playlists of upbeat kid-friendly songs, visit idealistmom.com/happy-you-resources.

16

Talk to Strangers

My friends and family will probably laugh when they read this chapter. Here's why: As much as possible, I like to spend entire days in my pajamas at home, going nowhere and talking to no one except my family. If there's a knock at the door, I never answer – even if I know it's just the UPS guy.

When I *do* leave the house, I wear a mask of introversion that clearly communicates to all who cross my path, "Talk to me, and you'll regret it." My niece calls me her "hermit crab aunt." Lovingly, but you get the point.

Last year after I reached my breaking point, a checkout lane cashier at our regular grocery store taught me an important lesson.

I never make small talk at the grocery store – or anywhere else for that matter. For one thing, I'm *horrible* at it. I can never think of anything interesting to say. And then while I'm busy trying to think of something to say, the other person already said something, and being preoccupied, I didn't catch it all. So I'm left just standing there, not knowing what to say, and feeling like a dummy while my cheeks turn from pink to beet red.

When I know I'll have to make small talk, my heart starts beating faster and faster as the conversation gets closer to reality.

On this particular day, I was in line behind two other people, and my heart had already started up the ramp. Then the first person walked away with her groceries, and my heart beat faster.

I looked down into my shopping cart, dreading the conversation to come.

But Then?

Silence.

I looked up. The cashier – a man in his 30s or 40s – was smiling and moving his hands. This confused me because I'd seen the cashier before, and he was definitely a talker.

I glanced at the customer. He responded by moving his hands. Sign language.

And I felt like crawling back under my hermit crab shell.

There I was, dreading "having" to make small talk, when a person not five feet from me probably couldn't chat with the vast majority of people he came across in his day.

The two continued talking, and I let this realization sink into me. When the customer left and I walked up to the counter, my mask of introversion had slipped.

The cashier smiled. "Thank you for being patient. I don't get to dust off my sign language very often."

I smiled back. Not a quick one to get the niceties over with. A *real* smile that crinkled my eyes. "Oh, no problem," I said. "Where did you learn how?"

I asked a question? Of a stranger? Who am I?

And we made small talk. But for once in my life, I was enjoying it.

When I walked away that afternoon, the weirdest thing happened.

I felt happy.

All because I talked to a stranger for a few minutes. I let go of worrying about what to say and how to respond, and I just talked. About nothing in particular, but for some reason, the experience boosted my mood the rest of the day.

Was It a Fluke?

I hit the books to figure out what had happened, and I learned that the experience I had was definitely not a fluke.

When asked to guess whether we'll enjoy chatting with a stranger, most of us will predict that the experience will *not* be enjoyable. But the research shows we're wrong.

The experience of a positive social interaction with a stranger does indeed make us happier – extroverts *and* introverts. Positive social con-

100

nections aren't just good for our mental health, but they're tied to our physical health, too. The more positive social interactions you have, the happier and healthier you are.

Even though I read the books and saw the stats, I still had a hard time believing this. And I probably would *still* be a stick-in-the-mud if I hadn't had that experience at the grocery store last year to reset my perspective on small talk.

How to Talk to Strangers

If you've read this chapter and thought to yourself, "Yeah, sure! This sounds great!" then set a goal to talk to a certain number of strangers every day, and you'll experience the rewards.

If you're like me and you stress out at just the *idea* of doing this, here are a few tips to help you:

- Make it a goal to talk to *one* stranger a day. You can set your goal higher later, but for now, start with just one.
- You can talk to people who walk alongside you as you walk your kid into school in the morning, people riding the elevator with you at work, the cashier or waitperson at lunch, and so on. You can even choose *not* to hide when the delivery person answers the door so you can have a quick moment of positive connection with them.
- Pretend you're a detective whose job it is to find out the most interesting thing about that person. Everyone has at least one interesting thing, so keep asking questions until you figure out what it is for that person.
- Still can't bring yourself to do it? Try making eye contact and smiling as a first step. Even that small gesture will increase the level of positive social connection you feel.

If you're not sure what to say, these example questions might work for you:

- What do you like to do?
- What are you looking forward to today?
- What's been the best part of your day so far?

- What's keeping you busy?
- What have you been working on lately?

This trick works when talking to kids who aren't your own, too. For example, when you visit your kid for lunch at school or go to their friend's birthday party on the weekend. Here are some questions that work well for kids:

- Can you tell me a joke?
- What made you laugh today?
- What's your favorite thing to do in the whole world?
- What are you the best at?
- What's your favorite game to play?

The Best Part of All

My new cashier buddy? The next time I ended up in his lane, I worked up the courage to ask his name.

Bobby Sunshine.

His middle name is *literally* "Sunshine." And so now, any time I find myself getting nervous about talking to a stranger, I just ask myself: "What would Bobby Sunshine do?"

17

Give

One of the most reliable ways to increase your happiness immediately is to do something nice for someone else. Volunteering is always great if you can swing it. But you *don't* need to spend every Saturday at the animal shelter picking up dog poo in order to get a major happiness boost. (Pro tip: If you *do* volunteer regularly, try to find something that uses your signature strength. See Chapter 7 for more on what your signature strengths are.)

Small acts of kindness increase your happiness just as well as big ones. This includes any small but kind gesture, from running to open the door for someone who has his hands full to writing a sweet note to put in your kid's school lunchbox.

Remember my new friend Bobby Sunshine from Chapter 16? Last time my husband and I were at the grocery store, we surprised him by buying him a chocolate truffle from the checkout lane.

We made his day, and we felt pretty darn good for the rest of our day. Although I guess it didn't hurt that we treated ourselves to chocolate truffles, too.

What You Might Not Expect

The most interesting part of the giving habit is that it works best if you *don't* do it every day.

When you do it every day, you get used to it, and it doesn't have the same impact on your happiness. For the best results, follow these steps:

1. Pick one day a week to dole out acts of kindness.
2. Aim to do five nice things for others on that day.
3. Carry out each gesture deliberately. If you get to the end of a day and search for five nice things you already did without really planning to have a Day of Doing Nice Things, you won't get a happiness boost. Set the intention of doing nice things for others at the *start* of your day, and after each gesture, you'll get an immediate improvement to your mood.

What to Do on Your Day of Doing Nice Things

Here are a few ideas for small, kind gestures, but don't let this list limit you. This is a fun habit to get into with your kids because they'll think of kind gestures you'd never come up with on your own.

- Give someone a heartfelt compliment
- Get the door for someone
- Offer to run an errand for your partner
- Let another driver merge into your lane
- Pick up a piece of litter and throw it away
- Pass along a book you loved to a friend who might enjoy it
- Buy an extra cup of coffee and surprise a co-worker
- Leave a sweet note in your kid's lunchbox or in your partner's car seat
- Give a generous tip to your waitperson
- Email a friend you haven't talked to in a while
- Let someone take the parking spot you were waiting for
- Smile at someone you don't get along well with – worst case, you'll make them wonder what you're up to and best case, you'll soften the hard feelings between you
- Make a Spotify playlist of your favorite songs and share it with a friend
- Pick up dessert on the way home from work and surprise your family
- Do your partner's chores for a day

- Buy a lottery ticket and give it to a stranger
- Let someone cut in front of you in line
- Bring a bag of candy to work and while everyone's out at lunch, leave one on each person's chair
- Learn a new joke and tell it
- Buy an extra item (or more) at the grocery store and donate it to the food bank

And of course, no acts of kindness list would be complete without...

- Pay for the person in line behind you at the coffee shop or the toll booth

Section 4
Use in Case of Emergency

18

Catch Yourself Before You Lose Your Cool

Remember: If your goal is to be like Mary Poppins 100 percent of the time, your goal is unrealistic. Nobody is happy 100 percent of the time.

No matter how many happiness habits you put in place, you *will* encounter small frustrations and annoyances every day. Probably some big ones, too. You can't deal with them by denying that you feel frustrated or annoyed.

Because bottling up your perfectly normal but negative emotion would make it *worse*.

In this chapter, you'll find a toolkit of proven tools to help you in that tricky moment when you're teetering on the edge of losing your patience. Because you need all the help you can get in that moment, your bonus companion workbook also includes a printable cheat sheet you can put somewhere handy in your home as a reminder. Download your bonus workbook at idealistmom.com/happy-you-bonus.

If you haven't already read Chapter 6, check it out. Losing your cool is a bad habit you can break, and that chapter serves as a foundation for what you'll read in this chapter.

How to Use Your Temper-Taming Toolkit

First, a word of warning: You must prepare yourself ahead of time – *before* the moment when you're about to lose your cool.

You'll have the best success if you follow these steps to prepare yourself:

1. Read through all the ideas in this chapter. Pick the *one trick* that sounds the most doable. We'll start with one, then you can always add in more if you need them. But if you try to start with several, you'll struggle to remember any of them in the moment and be back at square one.

2. Set yourself an **action trigger** by saying "If...then." For example: "If I feel frustrated, then I'll strike the magic pose that Kelly told me about, even though I might feel silly doing it, but it's backed by science and how will I know whether it works unless I try it a few times?" That might be a little on the long side, so you could try this instead: "If I feel frustrated, then I'll strike the magic pose."

3. **Practice.** You'll need to enlist your kids, your partner, or your mother-in-law. Give a quick explanation, like this: "I want to do better about keeping my temper in check when I feel frustrated. Can you pretend to do something frustrating so I can practice my new response?" You might be groaning at the thought of this, but I promise you, it works. These are all simple tricks, but in order to catch yourself in the moment, you must practice ahead of time.

4. Hang the bonus printable cheat sheet somewhere as a **visual cue** and circle the trick you'll be using.

5. The next time you feel your temper flaring, try your new trick. If you forget to do it, practice a few more times and say your "If...then" action trigger out loud again so you're ready for the next time.

If you find that one trick isn't enough to keep your temper in check, try adding another one after a while. Wait until one temper-taming tool is firmly in place before adding a new one, but feel free to keep adding to your toolkit until you find the right fit for you and your family.

Strike a Pose

Specifically, strike the Wonder Woman pose with your hands on your hips while you stand up nice and tall. This "power pose" is perfect for when your temper starts to heat up.

Does this sound a little hokey? I thought so, too.

But it works. Just striking this pose for a couple minutes reduces the level of stress hormones in your body so you can think more clearly.

Zip your lip, hands on your hips.

Do Three Rounds of 3-1-6

To catch your body from unleashing a full-fledged fight-or-flight response, do this:

1. Breathe in for three seconds. Count out "one-one thousand, two-one thousand, three-one thousand" in your head to make sure you don't rush it.
2. Hold the breath for one second.
3. Exhale for six seconds.
4. Repeat steps 1-3 three times.

As you exhale, you may notice that you feel a bit more calm. This is because this breathing technique stops your body's stress response and lowers your heart rate.

Label Your Feeling

Use a word or two to describe how you're feeling, starting with "I'm feeling…" For example: "I'm feeling frustrated," or "I'm feeling annoyed."

Remember that amygdala gadget in your brain that we talked about in Chapters 10 and 11? When you experience a negative emotion, the amygdala comes to life like an over-reactive car alarm. Then your brain *shuts down* to logic and interprets every little thing as a threat.

But labeling your emotions in just a few words tells the amygdala to settle down. A few caveats with this trick:

- Don't dwell on the negative emotion because then you veer into venting territory. And as we talked about in Chapter 4, venting can be dangerous.
- The phrasing "I'm feeling angry" is important compared to just "I'm angry." The extra word "feeling" helps you separate the emotion you're experiencing from your sense of self. It's a lot easier to overcome anger when you label it as something you're *feeling* in-

stead of something you *are*. You are not the hot-headed Anger dude from the movie *Inside Out*. You're just *feeling* angry feelings.

Do Some Math

Give yourself a random math equation to do in your head. Or speak it out loud if you want. You might think, "What's 57 plus 29?" And then you'll be stuck figuring it out.

This works because re-focusing your mental resources on a neutral cognitive task means those mental resources can't be used for emotional processes.

Say, "It's Not About Me"

Let's say you discovered your kid took money from your wallet and lied to you about it. Woo boy, I can feel the anger bubbling up just by typing that.

Reframe the situation by saying, "It's not about me. She must be having a bad day."

To be clear, the point of this trick is *not* to excuse inappropriate behavior from your kid. The goal is to keep your temper in check so you can deal with the situation in a productive way.

Because when you react like a sleep-deprived drill sergeant, you risk introducing fear and stress into the situation. When fear and stress are involved, your child's brain is flat-out *incapable* of learning anything from the situation. And my guess is that you'd rather your kid learn an important lesson than cower in fear.

Practice Mental Subtraction

This one sounds dark, but it's effective.

Suppose your kid is dragging her feet getting ready in the morning, and you're running late. Close your eyes and mentally subtract your child from the situation. Imagine what the morning would be like if your child weren't alive. Or if that's too morbid for you, imagine what the morning would be like if your child were away at summer camp for three months.

Whatever's bugging you, imagine it gone. This is called "mental subtraction," and it helps you remember to be grateful even when you're ticked off.

Ask Yourself, "Is It Useful?"

Before you say anything, train yourself to stop and ask yourself first, "Is it useful?"

If your toddler just tracked mud all through the house after you mopped the floor, you might be tempted to blurt out, "I can't believe you just did that!" Your toddler would hang her head and feel shame, but that statement wouldn't clean the floors, and it wouldn't help your toddler learn a lesson. Remember: When fear and stress are involved, your child's brain shuts down to learning.

Your Temper-Taming Toolkit

1. **Strike a pose.** Zip your lip, hands on your hips.
2. **Do three rounds of 3-1-6.** Breathe in for three seconds, hold for one, and exhale for six. Repeat three times.
3. **Label your feeling.** Say "I'm feeling..." and label the emotion, but don't dwell on it.
4. **Do some math.** Give yourself a random math equation to do in your head.
5. **Say, "It's not about me."** And then "They must be having a hard day."
6. **Practice mental subtraction.** Whatever's bugging you, imagine it gone.
7. **Ask yourself, "Is it useful?"** Before you say anything, train yourself to stop and ask this first.

19

What to Do After the Storm

I f you're reading this chapter, you need to hear this again: 100 percent is impossible. Humans make mistakes, and you happen to be human, I think.

Add the chaos of parenting to the mix, and of course you're going to lose your cool once in a while.

That doesn't make you a bad parent. Parenting is hard, and everyone loses it every once in a while. In fact, if you told me you *never* got frustrated, annoyed, or angry with your kids, I'm not so sure we could be friends.

6 Steps to Get Back on Track

If you've lost it, follow these steps to flush the bad mojo from your body and repair the relationship with your child or your partner:

1. **Get rid of the junk.** You likely have a bunch of nasty stress hormones coursing through your body, so take a few minutes to get rid of them and clear your head. You can jog in place, turn on some upbeat music for a dance party, or do as many jumping jacks as you can before passing out. Whatever works.
2. **Forgive yourself.** Research shows forgiving yourself for a mistake will make you more likely to learn from the experience. Say it in your head or out loud if you can: "I forgive myself."
3. **Forgive them.** Now it's time to forgive whomever you got upset with. Try this mantra from Chapter 18: "It's not about me. They must be having a hard day." This will help your anger dissipate.

4. **Apologize.** For the record, this is *not* an effective apology: "I'm sorry I lost my temper, *but* you should know better." Research shows a heartfelt apology helps repair a relationship, but no "buts" allowed.

5. **Promise to change.** For example, you might say, "I'm sorry I lost my temper, and next time I'll try harder to stay calm."

6. **Challenge yourself to five good acts.** The science shows that in happy relationships, you need a ratio of five positive interactions to every one negative interaction. After you've lost it, make sure to get five positive interactions on the books as fast as possible. Check out the next section for ideas.

How to Hit the Magic 5:1 Ratio

To repair your relationship with your child after an outburst, you need five positive interactions to balance out the negative experience of losing your cool. Here are a few simple ideas for what you can do to hit the 5:1 ratio:

- Give your child a hug
- Say, "I love you"
- Read a book together
- Leave a surprise note or drawing – in her school lunchbox, on top of her toothbrush, in the toy box, and so on
- Look into her eyes and smile
- Say, "I appreciate when you…"
- Tell a funny or cute story from when she was younger – or from when you were a child
- Ask her to help you with something
- Sit down and just play for a few minutes – no smartphones, no multitasking – just follow her lead
- Start a game of chase
- Tell a joke
- Go outside together – look for interesting bugs together, play catch, or hop on your bikes for a quick ride around the block
- Look through family photos together
- Queue up her favorite song and have a dance party

Section 5
Ride off Into the Sunset

20

Before You Go

You know what? A bad parent would never buy a book about how to be a happier parent. That's something *only* a good parent would do.

If you ever feel cranky, burnt out, or overwhelmed – or all of the above – don't you dare think of yourself as a bad parent. You're human, that's all.

Here's the good news. Even if you haven't read this book cover to cover, you're on the right track. Even if you lose your cool more often than you'd like, by purchasing this book you made a commitment to do better. And even if you're just working on one new happiness habit, that's one more than you had before.

Your family will be able to tell the difference.

If you take *nothing else* from this book, I hope you will incorporate a gratitude ritual in your daily life. That single habit has had the greatest impact on my own personal happiness, and the science is undeniable.

A grateful heart is what will save you on the hard days.

The truth is that in Chapter 1, I didn't tell you the *whole* story about the Day I Broke.

On that day, I lost it because of a fussy baby and a work deadline and my toddler twisting my hair into a knot while she tried to cope with a physically present but emotionally absent mother, not to mention a squawky baby sister.

When I hit my limit, I put the baby in her crib and left my sobbing toddler alone with a screaming baby while I hid in the closet.

And I screamed.

I felt primal, and not in a good way. What's *worse*, I knew my tiny ones could hear their mother losing it. Their rock, crumbling right in front of them while big scary emotions racked their little bodies.

My eyes feel hot writing about it again, even now several months later.

But here's what I didn't tell you. When I came back into the bedroom and scooped up the baby and squatted to hug my toddler, I glanced at the crib. And on the crib mattress, I saw it.

It wasn't there when I laid the baby down. I know exactly where it *had* been.

Three rooms away, on the kitchen counter.

But seeing it on the crib mattress now told me the story of what happened when I was behind two closed doors away from my kids.

A plastic teething toy.

My toddler, tears streaming down her own face, knew her baby sister was sad too.

She left the bedroom, went through the living room, and climbed up on a stool to reach the kitchen counter and get a toy for her baby sister.

She handed her sister that toy through the slats of the crib – an act of love from one upset child to another. It didn't help, but that's not the important part.

When I saw that pink plastic toy sitting on the crib mattress, I knew what had happened.

And the dam broke. All the emotion from that day flooded out of me, and I collapsed, exhausted and empty, into a *new* feeling.

Gratitude.

Gratitude for my child's gentle heart. Gratitude for getting to spend my days with these little growing people. And yes, even gratitude for the chaos of parenting life.

On the hard days, a grateful heart is what will save you.

Happy you, happy family.

A

Resources

As a bonus with this book, you also get access to a companion workbook of all the printables and worksheets mentioned in this book. This bonus workbook will help you find your *own* personal recipe for happiness in the chaos of parenting life. Just claim your workbook, download, and print at idealistmom.com/happy-you-bonus.

On that page, you also get access to a private Facebook community of your fellow parents where you'll find support and encouragement during your journey to become a happier parent.

For a handy list of all my favorite happiness tools and resources mentioned in this book plus additional books you might enjoy, visit idealistmom.com/happy-you-resources.

CPSIA information can be obtained
at www.ICGtesting.com
Printed in the USA
LVOW10s1819181117
556805LV00013B/1327/P